# The Winning Edge in Badminton

## Momentum, Match Flow and the Art of Competing

### Andy Wood &
### Alistair Higham

HAWKSMOOR
PUBLISHING

First published in 2022 by Hawksmoor Publishing,
an imprint of Bennion Kearny Limited.

Woodside, Oakamoor, ST10 3AE, UK

www.hawksmoorpublishing.com

ISBN: 978-1-914066-20-7

Photo Credits. Listed by page and image number. i[1], Suzy Wood. i[2], Hannah Behan. ii[1], Jack Hodgetts. ii[2], Etienne Jeanneret. 1, National Badminton Museum/Preben B Soburg. 7, 12, Shi Tang. 20, Carol King/Alan Spink. 24, National Badminton Museum/Peter Richardson. 26, National Badminton Museum/NBM Photographic collection. 29, National Badminton Museum/Peter Richardson. 32[1], 32[2], 45, Shi Tang. 50, National Badminton Museum/Peter Richardson. 52, National Badminton Museum/Preben B Soburg. 58, Shi Tang. 70, Ian Clark. 73, National Badminton Museum/Peter Richardson. 76, 79, Shi Tang. 82, National Badminton Museum/Chris Miller. 84, 88, 92, 106, 113, 124, 126[1], 126[2], 127, 132, 140, Shi Tang.

# About the Authors

**Andy Wood** has over 40 years of professional coaching experience. He is a former professional badminton player, Great Britain Olympic Head Coach and Team Manager, and Badminton World Federation (BWF) Expert Consultant. Andy was personal coach to the athletes that won the first ever Olympic Medals for Great Britain, Simon Archer and Joanne Goode and Nathan Roberston and Gail Emms. He coached numerous World, Commonwealth, and European Gold Medallists and remarkably – in the 2006 World Championships Mixed Doubles finals between Anthony Clark/Donna Kellogg and Nathan Robertson/Gail Emms (as pictured below) – he coached and nurtured all of the players through from childhood. Formerly the Director of Badminton at Loughborough University, Andy founded the Derbyshire Institute of Sport and was UK Sport Coach of the Year, and BBC Sports Coach of the Year in 2006.

*Left to right: Donna Kellogg, Julian Robertson, Anthony Clark,*
*Nathan Robertson, Gail Emms, Andy Wood, Hannah Behan*
*at the Olympic opening ceremony 2008, Beijing.*

**Alistair Higham** is an international expert on match play and momentum in sport. His work on momentum includes advising professional tennis players, athletes, and teams. Author of two bestselling books on momentum in tennis and football, he presents on momentum at conferences across the world. Formerly the LTA's Head of Coach Education, Alistair was GB 16U Age Group Captain, coaching and managing international junior players at the highest levels of junior tennis all over the world. He currently heads up the GB University Programme for the LTA and is GB Student Team Manager/Coach for teams winning Gold

and Silver Medals at the South Korea 2015 World University Games; and Silver and Bronze medals in Taiwan in 2017. In the 2017 European Masters, the GB student team won gold defeating the US College team, backing this up with a Silver Medal 2018 and 2019. He is also a qualified mentor working on the Premier League's EHOC programme and the LTA's mentoring programme.

*The GB student team after defeating the US College team to win gold.*
*Left to right: Julie Blackwood, Jack Findel-Hawkins, Jonny O'Mara, Pippa Horn,*
*Emma Hurst, Maia Lumsden, Scott Duncan, Barry Scollo and Alistair Higham.*

# Acknowledgements

Many friends and colleagues, too numerous to mention, have played a part in the discussions and ideas that form the basis for this book.

However, we would wish to thank, in particular, sport psychologist Ana Soares for her input on the psychology passages in the book and the following for their specific support, encouragement and, in some cases, critical comment on the material for this book as it has developed:

Martin Andrew; Emma Ault; Lee Bent; George Bevan; Ron Carter; Anthony Clark; Ian Clark; Gail Emms: Peter Gade; Mark Golds; Dr Chris Harwood; Joanne Higham; Andrew Higham; Jonny Higham; Geoff Hinder; Peter Jeffrey; Donna Kellogg; Mark King; Dave Lindley; Stefan Ljutzkanov; Greg Mairs; Jenny Moore; James Lumsden-Cook; National Badminton Museum; Phil Newbury; Jens Nyboem; Steen Pedersen; Elaine Pritchard; Keith Reynolds; Julian Robertson; Nathan Robertson; Ana Soares; Jurgen Van Leeuwan; Becky Warner; Justine Willmott; Suzy Wood; Ian Wright.

### Presentations and workshops

Keynote presentations, half-day and full-day workshops are now available. Tailored to meet your needs, both the content and practical solutions presented are ideal for:

- Coaches of Professional/Olympic athletes. Team or individual.
- Individual athletes/teams at Professional/Olympic level.
- Competitive county/club/student athletes.
- University guest lectures
- Business/industry professional development.

For further information, please contact: coachingedgeuk@icloud.com

### Websites:

www.coachingedgeuk.com

www.matchplaysport.com

# Table of Contents

# Chapter 1: Momentum, Match Flow and the Art of Competing

## The Mixed Doubles Semi-Final at the 2000 Sydney Olympics

I cannot believe what is unfolding in front of my very own eyes! How can something so amazing descend into complete devastation so rapidly?

I was the coach in charge of Simon Archer and Joanne Goode in their semi-final against Trikus Heryanto and Minarti Timur of Indonesia. Simon and Joanne were two of England's greatest ever performers in mixed doubles,

winning all the major titles around the world and – for a period in their career – achieving the prestigious honour of being the World Number 1 ranked pair. Simon has held the record for the world's fastest smash in badminton, and this symbolised his game, built on supreme power and aggression with incredible rear-court authority. Joanne was one of the toughest and shrewdest competitors of all time with a brilliant net game.

*Simon Archer and Joanne Goode winning Great Britain's first ever Olympic Badminton Medal in Sydney 2000.*

Simon and Joanne were going in search of the first-ever Olympic medal in badminton for Great Britain. A win here would guarantee a Gold or Silver medal and whilst, at this point in time, Trikus and Timur were favourites going into the match, Simon and Jo had prepared well and were playing the best badminton of their lives.

As the match progressed, GB were playing at a sublime level and were destroying the Indónesian pairing. Having won the first set 15-2, they were leading the second set 10-2.*

Simon was flying around the court, almost smiling whilst displaying supreme confidence, chest out, fist-pumping, whilst hitting harder than ever before and serving exceptionally well. Joanne was calmly confident, playing with immense conviction and lightning speed, capitalising on any half opportunity around the net, forcing her opponents to lift the shuttle for Simon to control.

Suddenly, a couple of fairly normal but significant occurrences in the very next two points, denoting a subtle change in energy and mentality left me fearing that it was going to be extremely challenging to win this match. (More on these 'two significant occurrences' can be found later on in the book.)

My nightmare fears soon became a reality, and what looked like being a nailed-down victory and a place in an Olympic final playing for Great Britain's first-ever Gold medal suddenly became a different proposition. The match immediately transformed into a totally different contest, with Trikus and Timur glimpsing a tiny light of opportunity. Simon and Jo could never reach anywhere near their 'sublime level' again, and Trikus and Timur went from strength to strength. Although Simon and Jo got to match point in the second set after a mammoth rally, they eventually lost 17-15. There was now no way back, and they lost the third and deciding set 15-11.

*(Note: This was in the previous scoring system, up to 15 points, where you had to win back the service before you had the right to score a point, making it even harder to lose a lead or claw back a deficit.)*

WAS THERE REALLY NO WAY BACK?

Is a match so delicately balanced that every single point can have a significant impact on the outcome? Even when you have a lead of 15-2, 10-2, and are playing the best badminton of your life?

This specific experience led to me frequently going through my match analysis files of not only the Olympic preparation period but of several years previously, and I was alerted to the number of occasions I had written comments such as:

- MOMENTUM
- TURN THE SCREW
- CAPITALISE
- OPPORTUNITY
- ZERO ERRORS NOW
- OUT OF THE BLOCKS
- KEY MOMENT
- IMPOSE

What I appeared to be identifying was a force or a flow, an energy within matches between elite-level international competitors, which became a crucial factor in determining the outcome of the contest.

My listings were so frequent and consistent that I decided to investigate further and examine this 'MOMENTUM FLOW' and the role that it plays within competitive elite-level badminton. Competitors in this category are finely-tuned professional athletes with considerable, but comparable, extreme levels of physical, technical, and tactical capabilities. Those competitors who can develop their 'mental skills', understand, recognise, and learn to control the momentum flow within matches can gain a vital advantage.

I knew of Alistair's work in tennis and football and following initial discussions, we decided to collaborate. As a result of working closely together over a number of years, we have built on this work and for the first time ever, created a badminton-specific text, designed to give you The Winning Edge.

**Andy Wood**

# Why do matches twist and turn like this? Why are they so unpredictable?

The answer lies in match flow and momentum. At the end of the match, the result is not always a reflection of the physical skill of the players. It is often a reflection of *how* the players dealt – mentally – with the journey of the match. It is a reflection of *how momentum was with them or against them,* and how they reacted to the situations that caused potential swings in momentum.

This book is about the 'Journey of a Match' and how it is affected by the flow of momentum in badminton. It explains how momentum can change the direction of a match, how you can control it, and how to make it work in your favour. The book is not about technique; instead, it covers the real problems that badminton players face, including:

- How to approach your matches
- How to get your game on the court
- How to raise your game
- How to hold on to a lead
- How to turn a match around

And all this can be accomplished through understanding match flow, recognising key moments in a match, and understanding what it takes to:

- Create momentum for you
- Maintain momentum for you
- Manage momentum against you
- Respond to potential turning points

But, before these problems can be solved, we need to know more about momentum itself and how to control it.

# Some key questions

## What is the journey of the match?

A competitive badminton match can last anywhere between 20 minutes and 1.5 hours, with the record for the longest recorded match currently standing at 2 hours 41 minutes. The shortest-ever match is recorded at just six minutes in length (bearing in mind that was with the old scoring system), but most official tournament organisers currently schedule 40 minutes as a 'best guess' on average match length.

During this time, the match will go through different phases. There will be times when one player or team has the upper hand, times when the other player has the upper hand, and times when it seems things are in the balance. This is because it is rare for players to maintain the same level of play throughout a match, especially as they are competing against each other.

Levels fluctuate for reasons we will explore, but are primarily: mental, tactical and occasionally physical.

As the journey of the match moves through these different phases, the score changes and how the players 'think they are progressing towards their goal' can affect their level of play which, in turn, can affect the journey of the match.

At the end of a match, you can look back and see the journey of the match to the extent that you can draw a line moving up and down across a page to represent it. During the match, as with any journey, you can also see possible destinations ahead of you, depending on your choices.

> The journey of the match is dictated by the phases of the match, and the flow of the match – including the powerful surges of momentum between these phases.

## What is momentum?

Momentum is at the heart of the changes that affect the flow of the match. Momentum is a powerful force, and when it surges, it can have a significant impact on the final result.

You can sense it when competing or spectating, feeling things going for you (or against you), or the players you are watching. Top players are always aware of its potential effect on a match; it can be like a fuel injection that changes the pace and sometimes direction of the flow of the match.

According to Briki and colleagues (2014), positive psychological momentum is experienced as an upward spiral, a period in which everything seems to go well. Negative psychological momentum is perceived as a downward spiral where everything seems to go wrong.

You see momentum at its most powerful during high-profile matches when matches get turned around. In the most extreme examples, one player or team can be totally dominant at first, followed by the opposition making a dramatic comeback. During this type of match, the feeling of an unstoppable force can be seen for both sides during different phases of the competition.

The changes in the performance of both sides are striking, presenting a stark contrast between the levels of performance seen across different phases of the match. The 'dynamic' of the match changes significantly, and it can appear as if the players are not the players they were! Commentators may even chime in with observations such as, "It's a very different team they're playing now."

Momentum – the feeling of things building for you – or against you – at times creating a feeling of inevitability about the result.

# Mixed doubles at the 2008 Beijing Olympics

At the 2008 Olympics in Beijing, Nathan Robertson and Gail Emms faced up to Zheng Bo and Gao Ling of China. Bo and Ling were the top seeds and, in the preceding months, had been on an extraordinarily long, undefeated run of success, amassing a series of major titles along the way. China and Gao Ling were also the British pair's old nemeses from the Athens 2004 Olympics, where they emerged victorious in the final 15-1, 12-15, 15-12.

The crowd was virtually full of Chinese supporters, and the continual, intimidating cry of "CHINA - JAI YOU" made it almost impossible to think, let alone speak!

Before the match, everything had seemed against the British pair. Robertson had undergone ankle surgery just six weeks previously, and the pair had slumped in form to ninth in the World rankings, just missing out, therefore, on a crucial seeded position in the draw.

*Nathan Robertson and Gail Emms.*

When the seedings were made, they had an extremely tough draw against the Chinese. Gao Ling was after a third (and unprecedented) consecutive Gold medal in the Mixed Doubles – while Robertson and Emms were the last remaining Brits in the competition after four British defeats in four days.

However, onto the court they came, fired up and raring to go! They quickly developed a 10-6 lead with the Chinese playing catch up. Confident and aggressive, Emms paced the court, keeping Robertson in order with that characteristic tap on the rear, pumping her fists, and relishing the contest.

With the first game won 21-16, things were looking good for the British pair as they opened up a 6-2 lead at the start of the second game. Naturally, however, the Chinese would not lie down. The middle game turned into a battle zone, the lead switching sides as fast as the rallies.

Returning from the break, Emms and Robertson were 11-7 up, but the Chinese orchestrated a comeback to win 16-21.

Watching the match was one of those occasions when you watched with your fingers over your eyes, clawing at your seat, pulse racing. In the deciding game, the Chinese pair grew in strength, and the Brits seemed to be losing their way. Emms lacked the pizzazz from the opening game, her smile gone, and Robertson looked tense. Soon they were 6-12 down, and the Chinese appeared to be running away with it.

Robertson won three massive smash points to scrape them back into contention, but as quickly as he won them, he lost them again, and at 12-17 the nine points needed to secure the victory seemed impossibly distant.

Somehow, incredibly, Emms and Robertson fought on, recovering from the six-point deficit to level the scores at 17-17. Clearly, in an attempt to break the run, China requested to change the shuttle. Emms and Robertson steadfastly refused; the crowd booed. With the 'lucky' shuttle in action, Robertson nailed one on the line, then another to take the scores to 19-18, then 19-19.

The crowd were on the edge of their seats. Then Zheng fluffed one into the net, leaving the Brits just one point from victory. The tension was unbearable before Robertson put every Briton out of their misery and sealed the final point with a series of power smashes before running deliriously around the court. With his arms spread wide, Robertson scooped Emms into the air to celebrate an awe-inspiring first-round triumph over the world's top pair.

As Nathan Robertson commented, directly after the match, "At 17-12 down, it is normally very difficult to turn a game like that around, and after a powerful smash, then we had an absolute surge of adrenaline and dominated with attacking play.

"It was also a case of this is our last moment and our last chance now. There isn't another opportunity to change this game around; it's now or never. One of those moments. We couldn't wait another 2 minutes, it was right then it had to happen, and it did."

# Perspective on the emotions of momentum (and the roller coaster ride of performance sport!)

By Andy Wood

Being right there, watching Gail Emms and Nathan Robertson courtside in the coach's chair, and witnessing this extraordinary event unfold, was one of the greatest and most memorable moments in my coaching career, as the 'Force' took over and everything fell into place.

Nathan and Gail had achieved something that recent history had told us was impossible – beating the nailed-on favourites, the top Chinese pair, in China – at the Beijing Olympic Games – in front of an almost entirely Chinese crowd.

At the preceding two Olympic Games, GB Badminton were on an upward trend with a Bronze Medal at Sydney 2000 followed by a Silver medal at Athens 2004. Here we were, in Beijing 2008, having just had this remarkable victory eliminating the biggest threat in the draw and being better prepared – physically, mentally, and emotionally – than we had ever been before. Surely, this year – 2008 – would be the year that GB brought home the first-ever Gold medal for badminton – wouldn't it? Everything was falling into place…

With an excruciatingly painful lesson, the harsh unpredictability of sport cut us down brutally the very next day. The young, emerging, but relatively unknown pair at this time, Lee Yong-Dae and Lee Hyo-Jung of Korea, played fearlessly with freedom and creativity to not only outplay us but to outplay the rest of the draw and take the Gold Medal. In doing so, they became the youngest-ever Gold Medal winners in badminton history. Who could have known that this would be the moment they announced themselves onto the world stage before going on to reside amongst the most decorated doubles players of their generation. Indeed Lee Yong-Dae went on to be World Number 1 in two disciplines with four different partners!

## What is momentum? (continued)

Having momentum is when the balance of power within the match is perceived to be with one player or team. When a player is described as having momentum, it means they are progressing in the match, and suggests this progress could continue or even accelerate as – once a player begins to gain momentum (in the right circumstances) – it can build on itself. Things can get better and better (and, of course, worse or worse with negative momentum).

This building, accelerating aspect of momentum undoubtedly comes from the scientific definition of momentum (mass x velocity) and causes people to draw direct comparisons with a snowball rolling down a hill, or something unstoppable like a freight train going down a track. However, the main difference is that – in sport – momentum can change direction and sometimes dramatically, a bit like that train track being up-ended and turned the other way around… suddenly facing the opposite direction.

In the train or snowball examples, there is no opposition to be considered; when we talk about momentum in sport, we should *always consider the opposition*.

Whilst momentum can be a tricky concept to grasp, even trickier to measure, and whilst you will have heard the phrase used many times (and it is easy to assume everyone understands what it means), it is often used incorrectly.

Momentum exists in all sports and is what makes them so exciting to play and watch. It is why the score does not always reflect the state of play and why the better/stronger player does not always win. Momentum gives sport unpredictability, which is why spectators stay interested.

> The flow of a match describes the direction the match is taking, and how quickly momentum appears to be moving the outcome towards one side or another.

Many words and phrases used in sport are linked to the *flow of a match.* For example:

- things are going your way
- stepping up a gear
- things turning against you
- lulled into a sense of false security
- holding it together
- can't do anything wrong at the moment
- things going from bad to worse
- took the wind out of your sails
- being up against it
- plain sailing
- having your back to the wall
- ebb and flow
- turned the tables

## Is momentum controllable?

You'll often hear people say that they don't think momentum is controllable. Indeed, in a recent match, a commentator spoke of "momentum creeping in and creeping out of the match" – as if it had a mind of its own and was not something that might be controlled!

If this is the case, how is it that some players always seem to manage to get momentum on their side when it matters most? It is not random – simply a case of certain players continuing to get lucky, like gamblers on a winning streak. If it were random, the law of averages suggests that simply being strong enough, fast enough, or agile enough would ensure sporting success. We know this is not true!

There are certain players who keep winning key points, who know *when* it matters to win a particular point or string a series of points together, and who can tell *how* and *when* to take action. They seem to possess an ability to perceive such things, and to time their moves so that momentum flows with them.

There was an era within the game when the Korean doubles teams (in particular, Kim Dong Moon) appeared – more than any other nation – to have an understanding of the control of the flow of the match. They appeared to know exactly when to raise the 'tempo' and when to work 'extra' hard.

I have lost count of the number of occasions over the years, when I have watched top doubles pairs compete admirably with the leading Koreans to the extent of having them in serious trouble. Suddenly, however, the Koreans will explode into another gear – for a short period of time only – winning their points in bulk (often through 4 or 5 point runs), thus killing off the game.

Lee Jae Bok and Park Joo Bong – both Korean and both international coaching experts – spoke a lot about this 'awareness' within competition during their time spent coaching in England. It is knowledge that many ambitious performers must work harder to acquire.

*Park Joo Bong.*

## How can you learn to use momentum?

Through experiencing or reading about the practical examples of badminton match play, you can begin to discover what it feels like when the momentum is for you, against you, and in the balance. You can explore how and why momentum switches; how to respond to turning points; and how to establish it, keep it with you, or regain it. You can understand why *fighting spirit* is the key and, more importantly, when the most effective times to use it are.

There are three reasons why badminton matches are lost:

1. Your playing level was not good enough.

2. Your playing level was good enough, but you didn't get your game onto the court that day because of poor preparation.

3. Your preparation was good enough, but you didn't make the right responses to game events, or the right choices relating to the journey of the match.

This book does not cover the first of these reasons (raising your general level of playing badminton); it focuses mostly on the last of these reasons. It focuses on *understanding* the journey of a match and suggests ways of raising your overall standard of competing during the match.

## Why is managing the journey of the match important?

Coaches and players should be aware that a badminton match is mostly 20% playing, whilst 80% of the time is spent thinking, reacting, and controlling mental and emotional responses (broadly known as mental toughness).

Mental toughness can impact your performance because:

1. Badminton is an open, fine and gross motor-skilled sport, and the environment is forever changing and unpredictable.

2. Badminton is a cognitive sport; players construct game plans and reassess strengths and weaknesses during matches.

3. The nature of the scoring system is such that players have to achieve a set number of points to win the match. They cannot build up a lead and wait until the time runs out. The aims of players must therefore be to control any anxiety felt – particularly in crucial situations such as points for and against, officials' decisions, etc. – in order to maintain the appropriate state of 'focus'.

4. Cognitive anxiety can also occur well in advance of a match, especially if the player has prior knowledge of an opponent's standard of play. A player's

perception of their opponent's ability, and the standard of the tournament, are often important factors in determining the player's pre-match state anxiety. High levels of cognitive anxiety within a match will usually bring about physical anxiety in the performer. The consequence is typically a loss of fluency and rhythm to the shots played, and diminished footwork around the court. Excessive muscle tension and disruptive irrelevant thoughts affect the ability of players to reproduce complex technical movements stored in memory.

5.  Match events will occur throughout the match, some of which can be challenging and some of which offer opportunities.

---

Former England International and National Coach Dave Lindley made the following astute comment in one of our discussions on momentum and an athlete's awareness of it:

"I believe some athletes are more accepting than others that they will not always be in control of the journey of the match. Acceptance gives them a better place to work from as they gain clearer thought processes rather than managing the emotional responses."

---

## Factors impacting a match

Many factors are involved in badminton matches, such that no two matches appear to be the same. This is because there are so many variables, for example:

- Shuttle type
- Style(s) of opposition
- Expectation
- Vision
- Locations
- Arena / Hall

- Temperature conditions
- Mental Approaches
- Shuttle speed
- Air conditioning drift
- Match events

If you are a player, you are likely to have had the feeling of history repeating itself in seemingly very *different* situations. This is because the match is always moving through the different phases, sometimes at a speed you've experienced before, sometimes at a score you've experienced before, and sometimes for other reasons that you've experienced before.

Managing momentum will help you bring together and control many of the variables that affect you during matches. This book explains why different match situations can produce the same feelings in a player. It will help you to make the most of whatever situation you find yourself in, whether you have just lost five points in a row, or need to serve out to win the match.

And it's not just in badminton that managing momentum is seen to be critical:

- When you play more and more matches, and gain more experience, you understand how to turn matches around and how to change the momentum of games." **Andy Murray**

- "Michael Jordan knew how to steer momentum. He was playing a different game to the rest of them." **B.J. Armstrong,** a team-mate of Michael Jordan

- "You have to learn from the game in the game. The momentum changes in that game as well, so it is not exactly the same anymore." **Jurgen Klopp**

- "At the very highest level, the outcome of a match is often directly linked to how well you play when your opponents are in the ascendency." **David Whittaker,** coach to the Great Britain Men's Hockey gold medal-winning team in the 1988 Seoul Olympics

## Why is momentum hidden?

The first place to see who has the momentum flow *should* be through the score, but **momentum does not always follow the score**, and the score does not always reflect past momentum.

This is because a match is a dynamic thing – like a moving picture – and the score on the scoreboard is more like a snapshot. For example, it can be 10 points-all in the final game, which would suggest things are fairly equal. However, like a picture taken of two people *neck and neck* in a race, it can look very different when you know who has the momentum, and is likely to get to the finish line first. For instance, the score does not reflect:

- Who has missed chances

- Who is getting pumped up

- Who is getting tired

- Who is starting to play better

- Who has been riding their luck

- Whose head is starting to go down

- Who is just beginning to work out the tactics to win

- Who has just broken a string in their favourite racket

- Who has the crowd on their side

Although it may not be reflected in the score, both players and spectators know with whom the momentum lies. You can sense when a player, who may have lost twice as many points as their opponent, has just gained the *upper hand*. Because it is a hidden force, people who don't understand momentum and how it affects a match behind the headline score, often come to some common but misguided conclusions (e.g., "He must have got injured" or "She must have played badly"). Many players underestimate its impact and believe the scoring system will reflect who has a higher standard of play. These players often say, "I should have won. I was the better player."

Momentum may be hidden behind the scoring system, but it does exist. You can learn to recognise it and learn how to control it - so the **final** score ends up reflecting that **you** were the better competitor!

# Key points to remember

- Momentum exists in all sports, and plays a big part in creating the journey of the match, which leads the match to a result.

- It is a tricky concept to grasp, and even trickier to measure, and whilst you will have heard the phrase used many times – and it is easy to assume everyone understands what it means – in fact, it is often used incorrectly.

- In simple terms, momentum creates a feeling of things going for you or against you.

- In academic terms, positive psychological momentum is experienced as an upward spiral, a period in which everything seems to go well. Negative psychological momentum is perceived as a downward spiral where everything seems to go wrong. (Briki and colleagues, 2014)
- Momentum does not always follow the score, and the score does not always reflect past momentum.

# Chapter 2: The Power of Momentum

We have witnessed, on many occasions, examples of matches where a far more talented, capable, and efficient performer gets ground down and eventually defeated by a shrewd, competitive warrior with less ability and half the number of weapons at their disposal.

We have seen many immensely talented performers coming out of the junior ranks, highly rated with numerous titles under their belts, full of confidence and accustomed to winning. The transition from Junior into Senior elite couldn't be that much of a big deal – could it?!! Well, the lessons can come quick and fast, even though they are certain:

- I can smash harder, move faster, react quicker, jump higher, and last longer.

- I have more deception and greater spins.

- My serve and return of serve are more advanced.

- Both my attack and defence are better.

The player ends up frustrated. "EVERYTHING I HAVE IS BETTER THAN MY OPPONENT'S...... SO WHY CAN'T I BEAT THEM!"

Compare the above to the shrewd, competitive warrior. They have:

- An unfaltering knack of picking out – almost instantaneously – the exact game style you don't like and applying it immediately, almost by strangulation.

- They put the shuttle exactly where you least prefer it within rally situations.

- They avoid your 'Preferred Pattern of Play' at all costs.

- They have no predictable or readable pattern(s) of their own.

- They are not interested in outplaying you or showcasing their skills – merely in making you play nowhere near your true potential.

- They read and anticipate every play you make.

- They are in your head and appear to take great pleasure in any visible frustration that you inevitably fail to hide.

- At the very moment they sense your complete bewilderment, they hit you hard. They almost sucker punch you with those limited weapons from their armoury, but by now, their impact is complete destruction and devastation, and the battle is OVER.

So, what is going on here? And what can we learn?

# The reality of competitive badminton

Badminton is a multi-dimensional, multi-faceted sport with endless variables.

Technically, you must master an infinite number of different stroke productions or 'shots'. You must be able to deliver them from an endless number of scenarios, within rally situations, under immense pressure.

Physically, you must develop aerobic and anaerobic fitness. You need speed (both explosive and progressive), speed endurance, and cardio endurance. You need to jump high and get down low to scrape the floor with immense flexibility and agility. You must master endless varieties of footwork patterns, each of which will be dependent upon an opponent's preferred style of play and ability to adjust tactically.

You need power to hit smashes of up to 400 kph and have soft, delicate, relaxed fingers to impart subtle touch and finesse upon a shuttle that weighs a minuscule 4 or 5 grams and which can be manipulated with the faintest of caresses.

You need vision – both peripheral and reactive – plus conviction and speed of thought to implement your decision-making and risk calculation.

You need disguise, deception, and cunning. Badminton has often been compared to a game of chess (relating to the number of tactical opportunities), and indeed to poker (with the need to bluff, control your body language, have nerves of steel, and take enormous calculated risks).

*Grace King demonstrating the immense flexibility
and agility required in high level badminton.*

The more you consider the above, the clearer it becomes that the outcome of a match depends upon many constantly adjustable negotiables, up to the point where even an extremely experienced, knowledgeable coach is often lost in trying to determine the most pivotal factors or reasons for a player's victory or loss.

Naturally, this promotes a common habit of reverting to default, reverting to coach education principles, and charting the obvious. For example,

- How many unforced errors?

- How many missed services?

- How many service return errors?

- How many backhand errors?

- You get the idea…!

Obviously, these are very important factors, but they are also – very often – not the real story. The trick is to take the above details and understand how match events can become significant enough to *create a change in the journey of the match*.

So, amidst the unpredictable, explosive minefield of a badminton court, surrounded by so many destructible weapons that enable you to kill or be killed, and the intense nature of cognitive engagement, it becomes critical to understand how the *less tangible factors* create 'change' or turning points within the battle of the match.

Often, parents, loved ones, and the nearest and dearest who support their players are typically the ones who are able to identify critical factors. They sense behavioural patterns and observe their player's emotional state. They may not be experts in strategy or technique, but they are experts in spotting their player's reactions to certain events and occurrences. They say things like:

- "Things were going badly until she saw the number one seed and potential next-round opponent losing unexpectedly on the next court - it gave her such a boost."

- "She was playing great until her old coach from two years ago came and sat down to support her opponent."

These are prime examples of **turning points** in Momentum Flow.

# Momentum and turning points

If we know that momentum exists, and we know what it feels like when it's with us, and when it's against us, and we know that it can change hands during a match, then the key question is: *when* does it change and why?

In a nutshell, turning points can happen when a player is boosted by something or when a player is distracted by something. If one player is boosted by a match event while the other is diminished, the bigger the change and the faster the momentum can swing.

> "The smallest thing could make a difference, perhaps because of a reaction or a reaction between you and your coach."
>
> Peter Gade

Some turning points result from predictable match events such as the end of a set, a break, or a missed opportunity. Others can come from the most unlikely of sources, some of which will apparently have little to do with the game. The one certainty is that potential turning points will happen in *every match*.

Turning points can produce momentum shifts and affect the flow of the match. They are always related to one of three things:

1. The actions of your opponent.

2. Your own actions.

3. External events that affect one or both of you.

Turning points are all match events. Examples of match events that could become turning points include:

- Mid-game towel downs
- Court sweeping – sweat patches
- Shuttle speed breaks – testing
- Foul serves being called
- Court repairs – re-taping etc

- Drive serving – getting away with bending service laws

- Bad line calls

- Net cords – for or against you

- Umpire's warning – yellow cards etc

- Crowd involvement – especially in Asia

- Winning or losing a momentous rally

- An opponent visibly showing an injury in-between points, but not in the rallies

- Missing an easy kill

- Distractions on the neighbouring courts

- Breaking a 'winning racket'

- Shouting or motivational outbursts from opponents

Unlikely turning point sources – which can still have a strong influence – might apparently have little to do with badminton (e.g., a player worrying about whether they will finish in time to watch their favourite football team, or a problem email from work worming its way into a player's immediate thoughts).

The one certainty is that potential turning points will happen in *every* match!

## The Sunflower Turning Point

The Swiss Open in Basel is one of the highlights of the professional tour, being an exceptionally well-run event that attracts a large, enthusiastic badminton crowd. Jakobshalle is an atmospheric, intimate stadium and one in which extremely well-heeled spectators turn up in their finery to enjoy the hospitality, interact with one another, and celebrate being able to watch the very best players in the world. It is a date not to be missed on the social calendar of Basel.

On this particular Finals Day, the Centre Court arena was especially resplendent – decorated with fine floral displays all around the court. You could hear the clinking of champagne flutes as the dignitaries enjoyed their hospitality in the VVIP BOX, which was centrally located in the middle but at the very top of the stand; clearly the finest seats in the house.

Donna Kellogg from England was locked in battle in the mixed doubles final, and was at war with her opponents, but particularly with the umpire – with whom she clearly did not see eye to eye.

It was the third occasion, now, that she was rooted firmly at the foot of the umpire's chair, arguing her case vociferously but to no avail to an unimpressed official. I could see Donna's blood beginning to boil; her cheeks changed colour as the rage began to overcome her.

Amongst the fine floral display, directly beneath the umpire's chair, was a beautiful golden orange sunflower. It stood proud and tall, head and shoulders above the other blooms. Indeed, it almost glistened in the lights.

Donna's fury could resist no more. In an act of unadulterated rage, one split second, and one perfectly timed blow with her racquet, Donna sent the beheaded sunflower spiralling majestically through the air at maximum velocity.

Time stood still, the crowd reacted in super slow-motion, and mouths opened in bewilderment with muffled gasps of realisation as the sunflower went onwards and upwards – seemingly forever – before appearing to plant itself firmly into the lap of one fine distinguished gentleman in the best seats, on the top row in the VVIP section.

*Donna Kellogg in competition mode.*

Although this was undoubtedly a stroke of the greatest quality, executed with superb technique, I am not sure anybody would have expected or predicted what came next, least of all Donna.

She got off lightly with her disciplinary action from the umpire (partly, I believe, because he was still in shock at what had just occurred), but her opponents completely lost their focus both in bewilderment and humour at the event. The crowd rather bizarrely warmed to Donna and her personality. Donna, herself, had relieved a massive burden of frustration and went on to play in a completely free and fearless manner, as her opponents drifted away. Donna and her partner went on to claim an astonishing victory.

# Turning point or blip?

At the end of the match, a potential turning point will either be a turning point against you, e.g., the moment when everything turns around and your opponent takes control; or it will be merely a blip – an awkward moment before the momentum continues to go with you.

In badminton, you may see players having match points, missing opportunities, and then crashing to a heavy defeat in the deciding game. Yet, you will also see the top players miss opportunities – perhaps when serving for the match – and then *still* go on to win the third game. Why didn't they also crash to defeat in the final game?

If inexperienced players miss an opportunity, they seem to panic. The more experienced, on the other hand, accept missed opportunities and don't panic. They are prepared to stay on court for three hours if necessary, and do not have a *crash* mentality.

This composed mentality was shown during the Japanese women's doubles partnership between Fukuman and Yanoa in their epic battle against the Indonesian pairing of Polii and Maheswari in the semi-finals of the Asia Championships. The match lasted 2 hours 41 minutes before Fukuman and Yanoa triumphed 13-21, 21-19, 24-22.

Throughout the match, rally lengths went over the 50-shot mark, with patience and resilience being critical elements to securing any point. To put this into context, Yonao and Fukuman had arrived in the semi-final having won their quarter-final over an equally staggering 1 hour and 57 minutes. Their early-round matches had also lasted a combined total of almost 2 hours. They certainly had the mentality of staying out there for as long as it was going to take… before they figured out how to win!

Turning points, however, are only *potential* turning points. They will end up either as a turning point or merely a blip, depending on your response to what happens.

For example, if you miss a smash on match point but regain your composure and concentration immediately, the match probably won't turn around. On the other hand, if you panic, change your game plan (e.g., start trying to hit clean winners to win quickly), the flow of the match could turn against you. In other words, **it's not what goes wrong that's important, but your response to what goes wrong.**

'Wise' badminton competitors are tuned into momentum and its swings. They realise that a match is a moving picture and do not get too excited when momentum goes in their favour, or too down when it is against them. They know it can *and does* shift. They appreciate that extra effort may well be needed at certain points.

An example would be Zhang Nan, who has calmly negated key turning points during matches and used them to his advantage on many occasions. One example would be during the Rio 2016 Olympic men's doubles final where – alongside the very experienced Fu Haifeng

*Zhang Nan*

– he came back from a set down and survived two match points to prevail 23-31 in the third set and take gold.

# Luck and turning points

Luck, of course, can play a big role in turning points. Not everything is controllable. At key times, a lucky shot can happen, but it is fairly rare (and rarely fair!). Some people put too much down to luck and are always claiming to be unlucky. For example, they will make excuses such as:

- "My string broke."

- "I just ran out of steam in the third set."

- "My opponent kept hitting winners on the big points."

Of course, they wouldn't say this if they had had enough well-strung rackets, were fit enough, and knew how to read the opposition's game!

However, luck will still play its part – so have a *positive attitude* towards it. When you are lucky, be thankful and make sure you examine your tactics carefully, because you might not be able to rely on luck again.

When you are unlucky, renew your efforts and bounce back straight away. After all, you don't remember lucky shots against you when you win!

# Momentum and the effect of the crowd

Crowds have a natural feel for the flow of momentum. Football crowds are particularly well-tuned into momentum; they care passionately about who wins and can often feel when their team is likely to score or concede a goal. You can almost always tell how well a team is doing by listening to a crowd or looking at the expressions on their faces.

Even more interestingly, the fans act as a mirror, reflecting back the energy of the team and therefore adding to it – either making things better or worse. For example, if the team is nervous, the fans get nervous, which makes the team more nervous, and so on.

Crowds can provide energy for their team or players through support. This is why it is an advantage to play at home. It is also why you can see such dramatic momentum swings when the crowds are at their loudest and believe anything can happen, typically in the most high-profile matches.

Interestingly, the Covid19 pandemic, which forced Premier League football matches to be played with no supporters in the stadium, had a huge impact – statistically – on the number of positive results for the 'away' team due to the nullification of the impact of the home crowd.

The crowd plays an important role in the match. Very often, crowd noise and behaviour (especially from your own supporters) reflects the journey of the match – emphasising good times, important moments, and times when it's not going so well.

The crowd can also be more active and can instigate a change in the match, whether it's unfaltering encouragement for you, or biased clapping against you; these things can impact a performance.

The importance of the crowd is easily seen in the bigger events when there's a larger crowd, and their importance is not lost on experienced international competitors as this example shows.

# The Showman

Earlier in the book, we referred to Simon Archer, who won GB's first-ever Olympic medal, winning bronze at the Sydney games in 2000. He was a master at controlling his environment and imposing his 'aura' on both opponents and court officials whilst recognising opportunities for performance gain.

At the very famous Istora Senayan Stadium, home of the 2000 Indonesian Open – some would say the home of 'World Badminton' – we had a great example of a match where Simon manipulated the raucous, passionate Indonesian crowd to be completely behind him; indeed, they adopted him as one of their own ensuring he had their full support and backing in the final, the very next day, against a Danish pair.

On this particular semi-finals day, the crowd seemed even more boisterous and louder than normal. We had witnessed this rather unwittingly upon our arrival into the arena when another England International, Donna Kellogg, was their first victim. There was no badminton on display at this point – the event hadn't even started – yet the crowd were at their seats, singing, dancing, and foot-stomping in anticipation of the play ahead and being able to see their Indonesian heroes perform.

We had literally stepped off the tournament transport bus in normal casual clothing and taken a few steps into the arena at the players' entrance which was in full view of the frenzied crowd. At this point, with her racket and kit bag on her shoulders, Donna lost balance over the step, tripped, and managed a remarkable few steps of recovery before rescuing what could have been a calamitous crash to the floor! It seemed that every one of the 10,000 spectators had spotted this slight mishap, and believe me, they were merciless in their mocking laughter, derision, and abuse, all directed pointedly at Donna. Testament to Donna Kellogg, and showing once again why she was a master at overcoming adversity – she had the last laugh as she went on to win the Ladies Doubles title alongside Joanne Goode, beating the top Indonesians along the way.

Later that day, Simon Archer, with Joanne Goode, had just won their semi-final against the Indonesian favourites and would now be playing the final the very next day against Danish Opponents Sogaard and Olsen. Simon appeared extremely emotional and animated whilst he engaged in a lap of honour, instigating singing and dancing with the raucous Indonesian badminton-obsessed crowd. He was handing out rackets and shirts as gifts to them. I, however, was anxious to get him out of the stadium, through the media requirements, and back to the hotel to start his recovery for the final the next day. When I finally found him amongst the crowd and suggested to him that he cut out the showmanship and depart rapidly to recover and prepare, he refused. He explained that this was extremely important, saying how he was playing the Danish pair tomorrow, (unusual for it not to be an Indonesian pair on home turf with a partisan crown) and that he NEEDED this crowd to be on his side!

Sure enough, the Indonesian partisan crowd were completely behind Simon and Joanne in the critical third game of the final, the next day, as they cruised to the title, beating Michael Sogaard and Rikke Olsen of Denmark 15-13, 11-15, 15-4.

*Simon Archer, thinking ahead.*

# Momentum and the score

Earlier, we saw how the flow of momentum can affect you, how it feels when momentum is for you or against you, and how it can impact your performance.

The *score* can also have an impact on your performance if you focus on it. The score is clearly very important, as the quote from Vince Lombardi (the legendary American Football coach of the Green Bay Packers), below, captures very well.

> "If it doesn't matter who wins or loses,
> then why do they keep the score?"
>
> Vince Lombardi

The end result often matters a great deal, and the developing scoreline is, therefore, a major guide as to how well you are progressing in the match. We'll have a look at this in more detail soon, but let's first examine the relationship between momentum flow and the developing score.

# The relationship between momentum and the score

The first place to see who has the momentum flow should be the score, but momentum does not always follow the score, and the score does not always reflect past momentum. This is because (as mentioned previously) a match is a dynamic thing – like a moving picture – and the score on the scoreboard is more like a snapshot. Try watching just the score of any match on the internet, with intermittent reports, and you'll see how difficult it is to know what is really happening.

Match Flow is based on how both sides are performing and takes into consideration how the score is progressing. The score will often reflect the momentum of the match, and depending on the scoring system, it may follow the flow of momentum.

For example, when the scoreboard changes regularly – as in basketball, tennis, or badminton – the score will often respond quickly to the flow of the match. But even in these sports, the relationship isn't always that straightforward because the flow of the match can be running strongly in favour of a team that is making a comeback, but currently behind in the score. You may see 5-3 on the scoreboard and assume the team winning has the momentum, but if the score was 5-0 previously, then 5-3 could feel very different on the ground. Therefore, the score is not always an indicator of the flow of the match.

It is less straightforward in sports where scoring takes place rarely or in an unpredictable fashion, such as football or hockey. Here, the relationship is less clear and the importance of capitalising on a period of momentum going for you, and taking opportunities to score, is clearly very important.

# The effect of the score on performance

Of course, the score changing over a period of time, or suddenly, also has an impact on the players. The final destination is a win or a loss, and as the journey of the match unfolds, the sense that you are moving towards winning or losing can have a big impact on competitors, creating an array of different thoughts and feelings, including:

- Complacency
- Panic
- Confidence
- Hope
- Despair
- Relief

# Becoming an expert competitor in badminton

Badminton experts are those who are aware of the journey of the match, and tuned into momentum flow and the different opportunities it brings. They realise that a match is a moving picture and don't get too excited when momentum goes in their favour, nor too depressed when it is against them. This is because they know it *can and does shift*. They are able to appreciate that an extra effort may well be needed at certain points. They are also ready for their opponent to make an extra effort at certain points.

Badminton experts are not necessarily those who play the game at a professional level. Everyone can improve the way they play and the results they achieve by becoming more of a badminton expert. Everyone can improve their badminton by becoming more expert in the flow of the match because momentum exists at all standards.

# Lin Dan

Badminton legend Lin Dan would be another example of a 'wise, badminton expert' – and not just for his undoubted technical and physical ability.

Throughout his career, I have lost count of the number of times I have seen him smoothly and calmly recover from a seemingly impossible situation, or suddenly accelerate away from an intensely locked and even battle with an extremely resilient opponent.

The best examples of this were (often) in his numerous enthralling contests over the years against Lee Chong Wei of Malaysia, where he inevitably seemed to come out on top. To have done this so consistently throughout his long career, spanning two decades, he has to have been an expert at controlling the moment and controlling turning point opportunities.

# Key points to remember

- A shift in momentum is often traced back to a particular point or match event – a *potential* turning point.

- When momentum shifts quickly in favour of one side, often after a significant match event, you can see a change in the performance of one side (often both).

- Turning points are created by the actions of players or external events. They can simply be *a blip* if players regain their composure immediately.

- Momentum surges can happen in a relatively short space of time, especially following critical match events known as turning points.

- There are windows of opportunity related to the score, and you can make luck work for you, or against you.

# Chapter 3: The Link Between Momentum and Performance

Matches rarely progress from *good* … to *very good* … to *great* … to *game over*!

Matches go through phases – through good patches, through neutral patches, and through bad patches.

To understand how the 'journey' of the match is created, let's look at what happens in an athletics race. During a race, you can see athletes staying with each other, athletes opening up leads, athletes falling behind or responding, catching up and overtaking. During the race, and these events, the action of one athlete can be affected by the other. For example, if one athlete tries to 'kick', then the opposition is forced to react, and this may depend on how *able* they are to respond either mentally or physically.

Beyond this basic spectator view, coaches and athletes will plan race strategies, some of which are more fixed. These strategies can include when to run their fastest part of the race, when to be more flexible, and when to attack based on the actions of the other athletes (e.g., when you see athletes 'bunch' and run a 'slow' race for the first part, waiting for someone to make the first move).

Of course, in a badminton match, the leads and gaps cannot be seen and measured in metres like they can in a race, but if you know the players and their relative performance levels, you can see gaps open and close in the match.

This is because performance levels change during the course of a match. Players are capable of playing 'above themselves' and 'out of their heads' for periods of a match, and equally of playing 'below par' during others.

At the start of a match, there is a variety of reasons which dictate the level players begin the match at (warm-up, current form, nerves, preparation, etc.), but performance levels will change during a match for reasons including how individuals are feeling in relation to the score changing, and how they respond to match events, to tactical changes, equipment failure, or the effect of physical changes.

> "You very rarely play a complete match
> at your top level."
>
> Nathan Robertson

As the match moves in one direction or the other, based on gaps opening up in performance levels, the player/team gaining ascendency is said 'to have momentum'. It can be that one player/team has only marginally got the momentum, or it can be that there has been a dramatic change – and momentum has surged in their direction.

Using the snowball example we gave earlier, a snowball is easier to halt and push back up the hill before it gains too much momentum. It's the same with the momentum of a match. Having this awareness allows players/teams to understand what happens during competition. The step *beyond* having this awareness is to look to control the direction or flow of the match – through actions – with the aim of gaining the upper hand within the match and winning.

Before we move forward to look at this, let's explore how it feels when momentum is for you and against you.

> "I sensed myself becoming bigger, more
> powerful and more intimidating whilst my
> opposition retreated and shrunk into
> insignificance."
>
> Gail Emms

> "I think when momentum is for you, you
> look to make eye contact more frequently
> with your opponent, you have positive
> self-belief, and you feel you can play any
> shot from anywhere no matter what the
> situation. You have the ability to think and
> react quickly."
>
> Julian Robertson

# How do you know when momentum is with you?

- You feel in control.

- You are relaxed, but your mind and senses are sharp.

- Your strokes are smooth, and you seem to be doing everything without any real effort.

- You move to the shuttle easily, and take it very early.

- Lucky things seem to happen.

- The shuttle and the court you are aiming for seem big.

- You time the shuttle with ease.

- You do not worry about losing points.

- You have a sense of inevitability about winning.

---

"When momentum is for you, you see solutions and not limitations."

Peter Gade

---

"I would say when momentum is completely for a player, they can find a zone where they are flowing, focussed, have clarity about their task, and are making good decisions effortlessly, which allows them to control the situation they are in."

Dave Lindley

# How do you know when momentum is against you?

- You feel unsettled.

- Nothing seems to be working.

- Your opponent is controlling things, even though you are still trying hard.

- Your legs feel leaden, and your movements don't flow.

- Your mind is in turmoil, trying to find a way out.

- Unlucky things seem to happen.

- The shuttle and the court you are aiming for seem small.

- You mistime the shuttle.

- Small things get on your nerves.

> "I feel like my rhythm has been interrupted along with a strong feeling of loss of control. I go on the defensive and seem to have very limited shot selection choices."
>
> Julian Robertson

> "I feel a slump in my body language, head and shoulders sinking lower, and I avoid eye contact with my opponents.
> I feel myself looking desperately at my coach for 'Help'!"
>
> Gail Emms

So, we see that momentum shifts can affect performance. Throughout the book, we'll use the battery graphic below to illustrate this change in performance.

The top of the battery represents your best level at 10/10, as there are ten segments. The colours moving up and down are the level of your performance compared to your highest level.

As you can see in the example below, the performance surges from 4/10 (40%) of the maximum to 8/10 (80%) of the maximum.

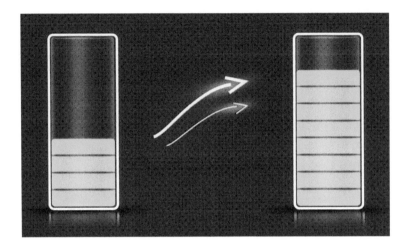

This surge can happen in a relatively short space of time, especially following turning points. And, of course, the reverse can happen if momentum surges against a side, and they are not able to control their response, as is shown below.

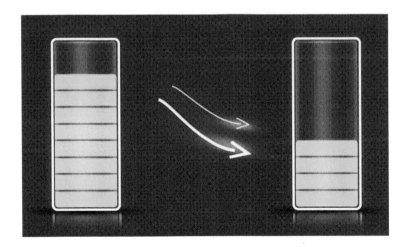

# How can you use this?

You're going to learn how and when momentum can surge, and how you can use it to:

- To finish off matches in style.

- Turn matches around from losing positions.

- Stop the opposition from building momentum.

In essence, you are going to learn how to gain, maintain, and regain momentum.

Let's look more closely at how relative performances can change during a match. We'll aim to illustrate how the gaps appear and disappear between competitors in a match. To understand this further, look at the graphics below to examine performance levels that can vary during a match.

In the first example, which can be seen as a *snapshot* of part of the match, the blue performance (Player 1) is at 80% of maximum compared to the orange performance (Player 2), which is only at 40% of maximum.

Logically and statistically, a static performance by both sides where one side performs throughout the match at 80% of their maximum whilst the other side performs at 40% of their maximum, would end in a predictable result. It follows that one side probably scored twice as many goals, twice as many points, twice as many sets, etc.

However, it would be a rare occasion for performance not to move at all from this position. As discussed, performances move as the journey of the match unfolds due to match events, match flow, and momentum. As the journey of the match moves through different phases, the score changes, and how the players *think* they are progressing towards their goal can affect their level of play. This, in turn, can affect the journey of the match and result in surges of momentum.

To further highlight the fact that performance levels move during a match, the graphic below represents a snapshot of the performance level of one team at three snapshots throughout a match: the start, the middle, and the end.

Have a look at it, and see if you can think of a match you witnessed (or played in) where this would have been true for you or your opposition. You might like to think about *why* the performance changed.

To build on this, and to understand how the performance levels of both sides can result in the overall journey of the match, the next graphic shows the performance of both sides.

Whilst we don't know any details about this match, look closely at each of the three comparisons, representing the start, middle, and end of the match. There are many possible explanations for these movements. Try to use your experience and imagination to utilise the information below to tell a story of this match.

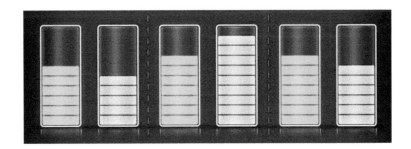

Using this way of thinking about how a match can progress, it is now hopefully clear how it can be likened to an athletics race where leads can narrow or widen, or indeed change hands.

When you are watching a match from a detached point of view, you can see a match go through these different phases; you can see when players are going through a bad patch and when the direction of the match has turned one way or another.

As an individual in the heat of battle, you may only be aware of the *feelings* associated with these patches, and not be aware (or accept) these phases have the potential to cause very different feelings.

Understanding that matches go through phases helps you to recognise that – at any given time – it may feel like the match is going for you, against you, or resting in the balance.

# Difference of standard

Of course, the above is accentuated if the initial standards are different. When one player/team is simply not as good as the other (e.g., lower-ranked, perhaps, because they are tactically less able), a change in both performance levels following a match event can result in a much bigger gap opening up.

If one player has a higher general standard, the underlying current of momentum will be in their favour, and no matter what the lesser player does, they will always be in greater danger of things going against them.

For example, if your *best badminton* is better than mine (in other words, if your 10/10 is better than my 10/10), in order for me to have a chance of winning, I need to play at 10/10 and require you to play at 7/10. If the match gets close and we head towards the end of the first game, which eventually you win, this is where underlying momentum can really make a difference. At this point, if you are relieved/pleased/relaxed and your level of play goes up through the gears, while I become despondent at missed opportunities and my level goes down as a result, the momentum can swing in your favour because of the distance between you at 10/10 and me at 7/10.

This is why the better player has the edge when things are in the balance. In other words, they have more room to raise their game. This is why the lesser player must *grab their opportunity* when it arises!

However, the fact that players don't always play their best badminton *all the time* explains why no match is without opportunities for the lesser player, and conversely, why no match is totally plain sailing for the better player. Matches do not progress in a uniform, consistent way for the better player; at some stage in the match, the better player may play under par, and the lesser player may play above par. If the lesser player is *watching for potential turning points*, then they will always have a better chance of pulling off a shock win.

In badminton, as in all games, opportunities arise for both players, even if one player is of a higher standard. The unexpected will only happen, however, if the lesser player keeps taking their chances and the better player fails to do the same.

In the example below, we can see that one player/team is better than the other, represented by the fact that the maximum level (100%) is at different heights. In other words, when they are at their best, they are not that closely matched, and the left-hand side has the ability to reach higher levels of performance; this player has more potential to go up a gear.

This has an impact on the match because to compete at the same level as the blue side, the orange side has to play close to their maximum level at 90% of maximum for a sustained period whilst the blue side has to only to play at 70%.

By comparison, the example below is a common one whereby the favourite side (blue) begins the match either cautiously or nervously, and the orange side starts fast out of the blocks with everything to gain.

By the middle of the match, the yellow side has dropped to 60% whilst the blues are at 80%; the gap in standards is starting to show and by the end, the steam has gone from the underdog's challenge as they realise the gap in level is growing and fear for the worst. By comparison, the blue side is relaxed and begin to show what they can do with no fear of threat.

This example is typical in many sports, and depending on the scoring system in the sport, it's when you hear the phrase 'the floodgates are starting to open' as opportunities come again and again for the better side.

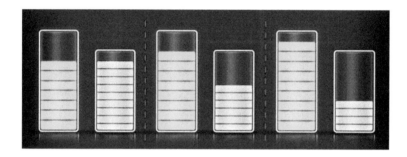

# Breaking down a performance to understand the link

When it comes to a 'performance', most sports split things up into four performance factors. These performance factors, together, are the makeup of your overall game and are a way of looking at the different areas. They are:

- Technical: how you execute the stroke production, movement pattern, spin, or hit.
- Physical: strength, speed, stamina, power, etc.
- Tactical: how you plan to win.
- Mental: thoughts, feelings, and emotions.

Because performance is split into four distinct areas, it can seem that they are all equal and each represent one compartment of your game. The reality, however, is that when it comes to what is *effective in a match*, they are not equal. And, as we will see, they overlap.

What factors can *you* control to respond to match events? Have a look at the list and choose two which you think can consciously change during a match to form a 'response' to match events. Think about which two of the performance factors have the capacity to lift or drop a performance by influencing all the other performance factors. And let's emphasise here, we're talking about a performance *during the match*, not about the standard going into a match which is a different discussion. Let's look at each, in turn, and what a player or coach can make a conscious decision to change during a match.

## Technique

Technique is less adaptable during a match. Players don't suddenly play with a new grip, develop new spins, or discover a new deceptive stroke. Technique is a pre-existing skill, and whilst technique may be executed with greater or lesser fluidity during a match, this is usually due to players tightening or relaxing due to mental factors.

Of course, superior technique can make a difference in a match because a side with a greater ability to execute, or deliver a wider variety of shots, will have more tactical options. And an individual player within a team with excellent technique can create impactful match events that can change the course of a match. The point here is that in order to consciously affect the flow of a match – *during the match* – you can't change existing techniques.

## Physical

The physical factor can have a big influence on the match and indeed the other performance factors. Players can get tired or injured due to poor physical conditioning as the match progresses, and overall performance can deteriorate. However, it's not something that you can decide to change during a match. You can't decide to gain extra stamina or become more supple. Players and teams can increase their intensity and demand more physical performance during a match, but this is a mental/motivational skill demanding more of *existing* physical skills.

Superior speed or stamina can give teams an advantage going into the match because, as a performance factor, they play an important role in establishing the overall standard. And as with technique, a burst of speed executed at an important point can change the course of a game. But, as with technique, in order to consciously affect the flow of a match – *during the match* – you can't change existing physical attributes.

## Tactical

Strategy, tactics, systems of play, patterns of play, and decisions to be made, are all adaptable in a match, and can therefore have a *decisive* effect on the performance level of both you and the opposition.

Whether it's deciding to become more aggressive and exploit the weaknesses of the opposition or to play a spoiling game that nullifies the strengths of the opposition (or even switching between the two), tactics are at the heart of influencing the performances of both sides and therefore the flow of the match.

## Mental

The mental performance factor encompasses areas such as emotional control, confidence, motivation, resilience, and concentration. For team sports, you can argue that team spirit (cohesion) and communication should be added too.

Whether it is frustration, anger, or loss of motivation or concentration, the mental area is perhaps *the most influential* performance factor affecting performances in matches. With body language and self-talk, players can reveal how they are feeling, and you can see a performance being affected by their mental state.

## Tactical and mental

*It's tactical and mental performance factors that are the key to controlling momentum.* This is because they are the two performances factors that players can consciously control during a match.

There is a strong relationship between momentum and the performances of players that works both ways. They are interconnected:

| Momentum both influences and can be influenced by performance. | Performances both influence and can be influenced by momentum. |
|---|---|

## Know your options

It is, of course, not that simple to say 'think tactically and be aware of your mental state'. It is important to take an individual approach to your own game because not all players are the same!

*Mathias Boe of Denmark, always thinking about his options.*

In the following two examples, Andy Wood reflects on the discrepancies in opinions and thought processes when analysing performances.

## Differing Expert Opinions on Feedback and Outcome

I learned fairly early on in my coaching career to choose wisely on the exact timing of delivering feedback discussions with performance athletes whilst in the competition environment.

So often, you don't have much choice as a courtside coach. You are rushing from match to match to cover all the players in your group, and you just grab an opportunity when it presents itself. As a result of this, you tend to fall into a pattern of delivering the post-match chat as soon as possible after the match, as athletes have another upcoming match to prepare for, and you can move on in your head to the next challenge.

Clearly, every player is wired very differently – mentally and emotionally. Each player has very different tolerance levels and different scales of judgement on personal and partnership performance. Each player is driven by a different priority on motivational forces: winning, fame, outcome, ranking, money, acceptance, and popularity, to name a few.

I remember quite vividly a post-match debrief that I undertook with a well-known GB Ladies doubles combination who had just lost a closely contested match to a top-ranked Korean pair. The British pair had played very well and had created opportunities to win the match, but were not quite able to capitalise on them, although they demonstrated progress in all areas of their performance targets. I had anticipated this to be a relatively straightforward, positive, and constructive debrief. What unfolded, however, was far from that!

One partner was furious that the match had been lost when they had clearly created opportunities to grab the win. One partner was very happy that they had both played so well and been so close.

One partner was furious that her partner could be so happy, even though they had 'LOST' the match. One partner could not understand why her partner was so viciously angry, even though they had played so well and improved in every area.

A very honest, vocal, and passionate discussion ensued where the two partners and the coach learned an awful lot about their performance, working relationships, and the importance of that dynamic.

The more positive outcome of this event was an agreement that the debriefs were essential and would not be delivered until a certain amount of time had passed, to allow for emotions to have subsided, to enable clear thinking, and to facilitate a critical, constructive conversation for creating an action plan. In addition to this, a 'Partnership Togetherness' project was established in order for everyone to best understand each other's personality traits (likes, dislikes, habits, fears, behaviour) when under pressure, and therefore have a better chance of getting more out of each other at critical moments of performance.

# Coaches' Disparity on Match Analysis

It was generally in team events like the Sudirman Cup, Thomas and Uber Cup, or European Team Championships where we would have the luxury of a group of us National Coaches sitting together in the spectator stands and analysing upcoming opponents' matches.

There would be idle, informal discussion in the stands about a player's strengths and weaknesses, and it would be followed, in the evening, by a 'coaches' meeting' where we would set forward a more formal tactical plan alongside the expert Performance Analysis support from our sports scientist at the time, Hannah Behan.

The disparity of opinion that could occur between a team of such expert, international-level coaches with a vast wealth of experience always astonished me. Most of the critical performance issues would be identified by the team, but the prioritisation of them and the ability of the individual concerned to digest them, act upon them, be inspired and motivated by them, varied considerably. I soon realised how critical it was for the exact tactical and performance message with which we were arming the player – before going into battle – to be personalised, within their capability, and delivered by the coach who knew them best of all. This would be the coach who would be sitting next to them, in the heat of battle, in the coach's chair.

## Tactical or mental?

Which is more influential? Can we find an order to make it easy for players and coaches to work with?

On the one hand, you could say that the tactical component has to be the focus in a match because the player needs to have a task to focus on (and do well). This task will be a result of decision-making which will be guided by your tactical approach.

On the other hand, where does decision-making take place? In the mind! And what happens if your judgement is clouded by frustration? And what happens if you know the task but can't complete it effectively due to nerves or because you're losing hope? Okay, so it's mental!

There is such a strong connection, overlap, and interplay between both mental and tactical elements that the answer is – as usual with competitive sport – that the priority depends on the individual and the situation they regularly find themselves in (or a combination of both).

Some competitors love fighting their way out of a losing situation, but struggle to close matches; others love being a front runner, but their heads go down too easily when things go wrong.

In the following chapters, we will examine the different ways that you can adjust your performance during a match, focussing on how to structure your thoughts and the tactical and mental options that are available to you.

# Key points to remember

- Very few matches progress smoothly from good to very good, from very good to great, and from great to game over.

- The flow of the match goes through phases which are:

  o When momentum is for you.

  o When momentum is against you.

  o When momentum is in the balance.

- Changing thoughts, feelings, and behaviours during these phases can greatly affect a player's performance.

- Understanding that matches go through phases helps you to keep perspective and understand that everyone experiences these phases.

- It's the tactical and mental performance factors that are the basis of any *match response,* and which therefore have the power to increase or decrease performance during a match in answer to match events.

# Chapter 4: Controlling Your Performance

As we touched upon earlier, experienced competitors make decisions based on an analysis of the current state of play, in order to assess options and decide on the way forward. This decision-making can take longer to learn since – to use this skill in the heat of the battle – you need practice. Experienced competitors have often developed this skill because they have seen different states of play on many occasions, and they recognise them quickly and make better decisions.

One key aspect of assessing the state of play is being aware of the different stages of momentum and adapting one's game based on what is known about these stages, what is known about one's game, and the way to respond appropriately. It can be a very individual approach.

## The five stages of momentum

When you are playing badminton, particularly in the heat of battle, it may seem as though there is no real link between the flow of the match and previous matches you have played. Yet, when we look at badminton matches more closely, it is possible to see the *same things* happening again and again.

In all kinds of different circumstances, comebacks are being made, leads are being lost, and hard-fought battles are taking place on courts all over the world, involving all levels of competitive players – from developing juniors to adult club team players to professional players.

Even though the circumstances are very different from the players' and spectators' points of view, what links them together are five basic situations called *phases of momentum*. The following five basic stages of momentum apply in all matches, but they do not necessarily relate to the score on the scoreboard:

1. When momentum is **totally with you**.
2. When momentum is **with you**.
3. When momentum is **in the balance**.

4.  When momentum is **against you.**

5.  When momentum is **totally against you.**

In matches, the flow of momentum moves through these stages, sometimes in a line, sometimes in a twisting line, which turns back on itself. It can move very quickly through the stages if something significant happens, or slowly if nothing significant happens. Either way, it seems to be in momentum's nature to want to move, especially if players are of a similar level. Given a bit of encouragement by either player, *momentum will shift.*

Reacting to each of the stages with the same high levels of mental and tactical application would be – in theory – the best way to cope with all these phases. This, we all know, is very difficult to achieve. To help accomplish this, however, it is important to have a fuller understanding of the challenges related to this task. Senior professional players or very experienced competitors have taken years to get to their very high levels of competitive effectiveness. Developing players, in particular, will regularly fail in one or more of the stages listed below while they learn.

*"I guess, through my experience through the years,
I'm about 80% aware of when my opponent
is more vulnerable." Peter Gade*

Let's take a closer look at these five stages and share some of our suggestions for how to return to your match-fighting best in each of them. These suggestions are based on years of experience of watching and being involved with high-level competition. We have tried to capture common thoughts, feelings, actions, and indeed misconceptions that can occur during each of the phases. Some of the suggestions relate to strategy and tactics, some of the suggestions relate to a mental approach (often reframing the situation), and some are 'match flow insights' based on logical conclusions from the work we have covered so far.

We fully recognise that some will land better than others for each individual, so these tips should be treated as a collection of suggestions – a menu if you like – where you take from it what you feel is relevant to your game. Later in the book, we'll introduce you to a more structured approach to help you decide on your own individual responses and how to measure them.

# 1. When momentum is totally with you

When things are going really well, you can be fooled into thinking it will continue like this – getting better and better – until the finish line. However, we know from comeback after comeback in big sporting events that things can (and do) turn around.

---

## Sydney 2000 Olympic Mixed Doubles Final

Let's return to that 2000 Olympic semi-final from the introduction, where Simon Archer and Joanne Goode were on the verge of victory and heading into GB's first-ever Olympic final. The momentum was totally with them before two fairly normal but significant occurrences led to their ultimate downfall.

Up until 15-2, 10-2, they had both been carrying out their roles impeccably with maximum effect. Thus far, the plan had been working perfectly. Simon knew that, in order to have his very best chance of winning the match, and keeping Trikus from controlling things, he had to serve low and consistently.

This wasn't the shot where he had the most confidence in himself, though.

Irrespectively, he knew that he should not resort to the flick serve, which was so often the easier option for him. Trikus Heryanto was an immensely skilled individual who – if given time on the shuttle – could destroy you with his artistry and deception. In turn, Joanne knew that she had to control the net, be aggressive, and not allow Trikus to use the net in order to get control of the rally.

---

Then Simon, having served low and brilliantly so far – and for some unknown reason – hit a flick serve to Trikus that he subsequently buried. Then, Joanne hesitated on one of Trikus' cross-court net shots for the first time in the match, and opted to attempt a net shot back below the tape (rather than committing to the kill and burying it).

These two events, at an unknowingly critical moment in the match, evidenced a minuscule change in mentality which was detected and exploited by Trikus and Timur, even though the momentum had been totally with Archer and Goode previously. What happened next was described earlier on in the book, but Archer and Goode never managed to display the same levels of supreme quality and confidence again for the rest of the match. They fought incredibly hard and even got to match point in the second game, but they failed to convert it and the match slowly slipped away from them.

*Simon Archer and Joanne Goode.*

Incidentally, Simon and Jo proved their warrior-like natures once again, the very next day, in the bronze medal play-off match. Having lost an unassailable lead and the chance of a gold medal just 24 hours previously, they had barely spent a moment together in their disappointment and anger. This time, they saved a match point in the third-place play-off to secure the first-ever Olympic medal for Great Britain! It was richly deserved.

## Maintaining momentum

Dramatic change can occur when momentum is totally for you, and you'll know, from earlier in the book, that this type of match event can become a turning point and momentum can shift quickly. As we recognise, though, momentum can also shift more gradually: gathering pace as it moves, catching the unprepared or inexperienced competitor by surprise… not seeing the warning signs until it is too late.

The areas discussed below all have the aim of *maintaining* momentum by understanding the state of play, and taking positive action to avoid some of the more obvious pitfalls or game plays by the opposition. Change can be averted if you:

- Avoid the dangers

- Understand the scoring system (it isn't football)

- Know how you got there

- Prepare to fight

- Reset

- Watch for a change in tactics

- Step up a gear

## Avoid the dangers

Momentum may switch, but at least make sure it's because *your opponent gained it*, not because you lost it. When the momentum is totally for you, do not allow yourself to get distracted.

This can happen in a number of ways. For example, players can get ahead of themselves and start 'kissing the trophy' or have finish line thoughts. This can be distracting and take them out of the moment, perhaps even adding feelings of anxiety.

On the other hand, some players may become complacent, which often results in a lack of attention to detail. They are playing well, their opponent may be playing badly, and it seems fine to relax and enjoy completing the win. Be warned! A big gap, made up of your best badminton plus your opponent's worst badminton, can become an increasingly smaller gap once your opponent starts to play a bit better and you drop a few careless points here and there. Your opponent then starts to feel better and play better. You, on the other hand, get frustrated because you know you shouldn't have relaxed, and you start to play worse. The whole thing can start to escalate and feed off itself.

Even if you are 15-3 up in the first game, and you have won five times as many points as your opponent, *do not be fooled by the score*. It may not mean you are five times better than your opponent!

## Understand the scoring system (it isn't football)

If this was a football match and the score was 5-1, then the team in the lead would be easing off, attempting to keep free from injury, saving themselves for the next match, coasting, and probably playing relaxed exhibition football.

But badminton is not like football, where there is a fixed time limit to the match and where a 5-1 lead means almost certain victory. There is no time limit in badminton, and there are potential dangers for the player in the lead because no one can be sure exactly where the finish line is.

Don't be fooled into thinking you've got a bigger lead than you have. A 16-7 lead suggests you've only got to win 5 of the next 14 points, and any 5 will do. Statistically true, of course, but if you play a few loose points and your opponent gets encouraged and gains momentum, 16-13 will feel very different, particularly if you've missed an easy smash or two.

## Know how you got there

If you relax without knowing *why* you have the lead, you probably won't notice if anything changes. It's like getting the first answer right in your maths exam without knowing why, and being pleased with yourself nonetheless. You are likely to pay the price for your complacency.

Are you winning because you are controlling the tactics, or because you have been winning close points on one-off happenings against the run of play? For example, these might be net cords, bad calls by the umpire, or the first on the line smashes you hit this year! If the latter is true, then you should still be guarding against a flow change because these things are not completely controllable by you.

On the other hand, if you got to 15-5 up because your own tactics and superior play are working, you can relax a little (but not too much) because *you understand why* you are 15-5 ahead.

## Prepare to fight

You have to be prepared to fight to keep your lead. People can play better when behind; they can relax and play as if they have nothing to lose. They are also likely to change tactics as a last roll of the dice.

It may seem illogical, but at 18-12 up, you must be alert to these possibilities and therefore prepared to increase your own level of intensity and to work even harder. **Fighting spirit is not only needed when you are behind.** It is not comforting to know you may have to work harder when you've played some of your best badminton to reach this position, but it is the best way of ensuring that the momentum remains with you.

This is particularly true if you are close to winning the match. Focussed, competitive players will not go down without a fight – so be prepared to fight and be surprised if you don't have to. It's always better that way round – **hope for the best, but prepare for the worst.**

## Reset

The start of a new game – having won the previous game – is an opportunity for a reset to occur. This facilitates a change in focus and intensity.

Winning the first three points of the game is important at any time, but it is sometimes neglected when you are in the lead. When players are losing, they can lose hope quickly. The first few points of each game, particularly when you are playing a tired opponent, can encourage or discourage them at a time when they may be clinging onto any last signs of hope before they lose heart. This is also true for every mid-game interval at 11 points. It is a good habit to try to focus on. Set your own target here, and be comfortable with it. You may feel three points is too much, and the sense of disappointment if you don't achieve it outweighs the value of the target. You may choose one point or two, but either way, focus on your response to the interval.

## Watch for a change in tactics

Knowing how you got to *where you are* allows you to spot a change in the tactics of your opponent more quickly.

You may not have the immediate answer to your opponent's new tactics, but (at least) don't be caught out by realising they've changed them once they have drawn level.

If your opponent does change tactics, be sure to renew your efforts. Players who are losing change tactics because they have to. Everyone knows you don't change a winning game, but you do change a losing game. A common time for your opponent to change their tactics is the start of the second game. This is a natural time for a review to take place by both players. Whatever they change to, it's going to be their Plan B (because nobody would keep Plan A up their sleeve to change to in an emergency!), and therefore they are unlikely to stick to Plan B for long if you renew your focus and combat them well.

## Step up a gear

As long as you are aware of the above, now is the time you can gamble, take more risks, and try to step up a gear by relaxing. You probably have a cushion in the lead and can use this to find higher levels of play. It may depend on the score.

You can use the cushion of a lead to try to kill off the match if it's getting near the end. Or if it's not near the end, you may step up and play so well that your opponent thinks you are invincible, which in turn may have a big effect on the outcome of the match.

Some players make it a policy to step up every time they have created some daylight between them and their opponent, for this reason. Not a change of tactics, per se, but consciously stepping the level up and playing with freedom.

It's also a good time to *vary* your game. You are feeling good, so variations are more likely to work. Not only this, your opponent won't realise that you vary things only when the momentum is totally with you; they'll just remember that you may/can vary your play. As long as it is a calculated gamble, and you are ready to return to your earlier tactics quickly if required, then go for it. Take the shuttle earlier, hit it harder, or change the patterns of play!

The time players slip up when doing this is when they keep gambling for too long and keep giving their opponent cheap points trying to hit winners… sometimes to make up for the ones they missed! Cheap points, of course, are exactly what your opponent wants when they are well behind… it's easier climbing steep hills with a helping hand.

Mentally, you can afford to step up as well. The best way to do this is to relax your mind and allow yourself the freedom of going for your shots. An international coach from Denmark once told me: "Talent is inside you. It stays trapped inside when your mind and body are tense. It can only flow out when you are relaxed."

This relaxed state of focus makes it possible to take your game to higher levels. Many badminton players and athletes have experienced it, and it has become known as *being in the zone* or *playing out of your head*.

When your mind is clear, you are capable of very high levels of badminton. Just think about how many perfect winners you have hit in practice. To relax your mind, and let things happen when the points are live, takes practice and courage, but it can be done.

When the momentum is totally with you, it's a good time to begin learning about this type of stepping up a gear.

---

## Nathan Robertson – Tactical Thinking: The Dangers of Over-thinking

Former World Champion and World No. 1 Nathan Robertson had an extraordinary ability to assess tactical plans and analyse – with clarity – who was doing what to whom during the constant battle of tactical wits between opponents. Not only that, he had the variety and confidence to adapt and adjust rapidly to any given tactical situation.

Mixed doubles is generally credited as being the most tactically complex of the five disciplines in badminton, and these natural abilities served him and his partner Gail Emms extremely well the vast majority of the time. On rare occasions, however, his cognitive activation spiralled into overload and from the coach's chair at the back of the court I could almost hear the whirring noise of the cogs turning in Nathan's head! He was trying to create a new plan for his previous plan, which had replaced his original plan before implementing his next plan. Nathan was 'overthinking' and sinking into the depths of complication and cognitive blockage!

I would receive a look of desperation and confusion from Gail as Nathan would try to communicate his thoughts to her in-between points. Immediately, 'keyword calls' from the coach's chair would be along the lines of "Simplify", "Basics", "Early and Simple", "Just play the crazy game".

Incidentally, "The Crazy Game" is a phrase that I have found myself using on a daily basis, as a coach, when preparing athletes for the session ahead, generally in and around the warm-up/preparation period. "The Crazy Game" hints at words like eccentric, enthusiastic, and fun. The aim is to invoke a smile and a certain freedom and joy in what lies ahead – hopefully inspiring creativity and freedom of thought in what is about to transpire.

**Key points to remember when momentum is totally with you**

- Avoid the dangers
- Understand the scoring system (it isn't football)
- Know how you got there
- Prepare to fight
- Reset
- Watch for a change in tactics
- Step up a gear

# 2. When momentum is with you

There are many similarities between this stage and the previous stage. However, potential turning points can be more important when momentum is with you because you have less of a cushion to fall back on. In the previous stage (i.e., when momentum is totally with you), you have longer – though, as we saw, not too long – to get your attitude right because your opponent has a lot of ground to make up.

## Put the radar on

When momentum is with you, if you don't spot a potential turning point and react to it, things could turn against you. Therefore, you need to have your *turning points radar* switched on.

Potential turning points were covered in Chapter One. But remember, they always relate to one of three things:

- The actions of your opponent.

- Your own actions.

- External events that affect one or both of you (including the scoring system).

They all have one thing in common: the potential to cause a change in the balance of the mental state of one player or the other, which then causes a change in the momentum flow of the match.

When you spot a potential turning point, you need to be ready to raise your intensity and effort because potential turning points need not turn into actual turning points.

## Understand how to respond to potential turning points against you

Potential turning points are always things that are able to depress or boost you or your opponent. When you have the lead, they usually take the form of **distractions to you and/or positive changes by your opponent.**

When potential turning points occur, your response is what counts. If a player reacts

negatively, you can sense the momentum beginning to turn. Even non-badminton playing spectators can sense this feeling – they can relate to the human reaction to something going wrong and the implications of this. They sense it is the player's response immediately after a potential turning point that determines how big an effect it will have on the match.

Chris Langridge (European champion and bronze medallist at

*England's Chris Langridge and Marcus Ellis.*

the Rio Olympic Games in men's doubles) is an example of a player who often benefited from this double change in energy. He brought about match flow changes by having discussions or interactions with umpires or court officials. These incidents usually ended up with him feeling fired up, mentally, with his opponent having gone cold physically and distracted by the long interruption.

The real dynamite for changing momentum is when both distractions to you and positive changes to your opponent happen together and feed off each other. **It is your job never to let them happen together when you have the lead.**

You may not be able to control your opponent's attitude, but you can control yours.

If a turning point has just happened against you, and your opponent suddenly raises their energy/game because they feel good, you have to be prepared to quickly raise your energy/game too, so your opponent doesn't get the momentum. It's like being in a running race, and your opponent decides to kick – *you have to respond*. If you do this well, then your opponent may lose heart if their best attempt to catch you up has failed.

If you learn to react to disappointing events (e.g., potential turning points) with the untypical reaction of not letting them get you down, then you will at least be lessening the potential swing to your opponent.

Part of getting this attitude right happens before you go onto court. Think for a minute about how many perfect matches you have played. Most of the players I know have played hundreds of matches but can only ever recall a few perfect matches. Of all the things we don't know about your next match, we can at least be sure of one thing – at some stage, something will go wrong. Therefore, prepare your mind for something going wrong – make sure you are psyched up for any potential turning points against you, so that you are ready to respond positively.

With the right attitude, you can turn potential turning points against you in your favour. Win a rally, for example, by counter-attacking and recovering from a tough situation (a net cord is a good example of this). You may have had something go wrong to have a match point against you, but if you win it and go on to win the game, it actually creates more momentum for you than just winning a game in a straightforward manner.

Key factors that will determine your ability to control potential turning points against you include:

- Keeping control of your body language
- Dealing with gamesmanship
- Keeping the match running

- Choking – your attitude towards it

# Embrace the Challenge

Our GB athletes returned from the Olympic Games in Atlanta in 1996 with just one gold medal. Much changed in British sport over the next four years leading into the Sydney 2000 Olympic Games.

The introduction of the National Lottery, conceived under John Major's leadership, had a profound impact across every aspect of high-performance sport in the UK. Many athletes who had previously needed to work part-time to fund their passion were suddenly being paid to train full-time and every aspect of the UK's high-performance ecosystem was being professionalised.

Internationally-renowned expert consultants devised strategies to address the physiological challenges of acclimatisation as well as the 'Team Dynamics' of a multi-sport Games, and how to maximise 'Togetherness' across a huge number of athletes accustomed to competing purely for themselves within their specific sports. As part of this programme, 23 Olympic Sport Team Leaders and Performance Directors met up on a regular basis to coordinate their strategic planning.

At one such planning meeting, involving Olympic Team Leaders and select potential medallist Olympic athletes, I remember lengthy discussions on all of the upcoming challenges and problems that Team GB had to overcome to manage the logistics of a modern Olympic Games and the world's largest, peacetime gathering of people. The boxer Audley Harrison had heard enough of the negativity at one of these meetings, and he walked onto the stage with his arms in the air as a symbol of power, with his 6ft 8inch, frame and stated, "I thrive on Adversity."

It was an uplifting and invigorating statement from someone who, sure enough, went on to not only claim the gold medal, but inspire those GB Team members around him.

## Body language

Body language is important at every stage because even if you can't control your energy, you need to at least control how it looks to your opponent. This is true when momentum is for you, but a match event could become a turning point depending on your reaction to it and how it is perceived by the opposition. If they get a boost from what's happening in the match (e.g., a big winner, a service fault, an unexpected missed smash), you don't want to double this boost by letting them see you are downcast by it.

It is vital to remember that *a potential turning point will end up as a turning point, or merely a blip, depending on your response to what happens.* **It's not what goes wrong, but your response to what goes wrong that matters.** You have to be mentally prepared to renew your efforts if you slip up when in the lead. Remember that *fighting spirit is not only needed when you are behind.*

## Dealing with gamesmanship

Players who have the momentum against them and feel they are running out of time sometimes use gamesmanship. This is because players who are losing get more desperate. It is basically an attempt to cause a distraction, so you lose your focus. It often works because you tend to relax a bit when things are going for you and can get distracted more easily.

Understanding what these players are trying to do can help you keep your focus. Gamesmanship is all about disruption; it usually involves, at best, bending the rules and, at worst, cheating. This can cause feelings of unfairness that can divert some of your mental energy from the game itself.

Players who resort to gamesmanship usually pretend to be ignorant of the problem they are causing while knowing there are no rules that can deal with it effectively. This adds to the feeling of unfairness and increases your distraction.

Matches can be won or lost either on a badminton or non-badminton (e.g., gamesmanship) basis. It's like having two battlefields on which two different clashes are fought. On one battlefield, there is the badminton game; on the other battlefield is the gamesmanship game.

If your opponent can't win on the badminton battlefield, they might try to entice you onto the gamesmanship battlefield, particularly on a big point. Do not be tempted to go there. Winning battles is a lot to do with who gets to choose the battlefield. If your opponent is trying gamesmanship, they have probably found it to work before, and have been practising on that battlefield for a long time. It is their home ground.

Therefore, stay on your winning battlefield – the badminton battlefield.

If it's a questionable line call, don't get involved in arguing if you are in the lead and you know it will distract you. Make your point strongly and keep the match about badminton by refocusing solely on the game itself.

Beware! There are many forms of gamesmanship including:

## Towel down breaks

These can give your opponent time to recover and let you go off the boil, either by allowing time for you to be distracted mentally, or by ensuring you *go cold* physically. Be sure to keep warm. Use the time to review which tactics are working and be ready for your opponent to renew their efforts when they come back. It's a good idea to head off for a towel down break when your opponent does – so as not to be left going cold.

## Bad line calls

If you do not have an umpire, and you receive a bad line call, it is very easy to be distracted. Here is an example of how you can react positively to a bad line call:

- Walk to the net and calmly but strongly ask your opponent if they are sure it was out.

- If they say yes, ask how far out it was.

- Say you thought it was in, and ask if they are prepared to play the point again.

- If they are not, continue with the game and put your focus into concentrating on the badminton. This is crucial because you do not want long interruptions when you have the momentum.

If you have an umpire, you can also query the call but then continue soon after for the same reasons.

Because of the time it takes, it may *not be worth* getting the referee to come to the court when you have the momentum with you, as the wind may go out of your sails.

## Biased clapping

When you make a mistake, you naturally feel down. When your opponent's supporters clap your mistakes, they hope to make you feel worse, to the point of distracting you from the game. Remember this, and don't fall into the trap of glaring at them or appealing to their sense of fairness. Stay focussed on the badminton.

Whatever you are facing, keep in mind that things could be worse! Here are a couple of examples of what actually happened at international level.

# Maximising Home Advantage

An example from Andy Wood

Something quite extraordinary happened to me at an International Exhibition match in a major Asian city. Having been announced onto court for the opening match, I noticed – whilst in the middle of the three-minute knock-up – that both stands at the sides of the show court were full of spectators, and the atmosphere was building nicely. The two stands at the ends of the court, however, were different. One of them was completely full and the other one was completely empty.

I remember thinking how odd that was, but didn't give it much more attention as I was really trying to focus on the match ahead, and getting a really intense and quality pre-match warm-up completed.

The umpire announced 'time', signalling the end of the knock-up and for the coin toss to commence. This was the moment at which it became clear to the crowd which end my partner and I – the visiting team – would be facing. The crowd overall were extremely quiet in anticipation of the start of the match, but the peace was broken by a loud shuffling of footsteps and seats clanging as about two hundred spectators left their seats altogether at the same time, from the one full stand at the end of the court, and relocated themselves to the empty stand at the other end of the arena.

They were now directly facing my partner and me.

It suddenly dawned on me that they were all wearing white shirts. The effect was a blinding white screen making it virtually impossible for us to locate the white shuttle when in play. Our opponents, however, now faced a completely empty stand with near-perfect vision of the shuttle in play. I remember being quite astounded at this blatant attempt to maximise home country advantage, and being so perturbed that it completely unsettled me at the start of the match. It certainly did not make me feel any better when, at the end of the first game, we changed ends and so did the two hundred or so white-shirted spectators, so that once again, they were directly in front of us! I never fully recovered from this and we sunk to defeat in what was a very winnable match!

# Another Instance of Maximising Home Country Advantage

Air conditioning in badminton arenas can be a blessing, particularly for spectators in hot Asian climates. But it can also be a huge hurdle for Europeans and particularly Brits to overcome. We are certainly not accustomed to working with it in any of our performance and preparation environments in the UK, where the temperatures are never warm enough.

I remember an old atmospheric stadium in Malaysia where the playing temperature was so severe, and the venue had no air conditioning facility. In each of the coaching breaks, after every 11 points, I had to take replacement socks and shoes onto court – our players were literally 'squelching' around the court with flooded footwear. We also had to use ice wraps to put around the players' bodies to get their core body temperatures down, even if only temporarily.

More frequently, however, our challenge was in overcoming the air conditioning systems as the shuttlecock is so light that it is significantly impacted by any slight drift of air or change in atmosphere. It took us an awful lot of preparation time to figure out which way the drift of air was flowing – am I hitting against the wind or am I with the wind? Do I have a cross-drift or is the shuttle holding up at the net? The Asian players are generally far more skilled at assessing and making these adjustments effectively, as they have prepared from an early age in such environments.

You can imagine our panic, then, having finally mastered the air conditioning – and having produced a solid, efficient, error-free display to stand on the edge of a fine victory – when the airflow, drift, and wind suddenly completely changed and we felt like we were caught in the middle of a tornado! In this case, it appeared as though somebody had mysteriously cranked the air conditioning switch to 'full throttle' in a last-ditch attempt to derail us from almost-certain victory.

# Keeping the match running

When you have the momentum with you, don't create distractions against yourself. Keep the match running. When things are going your way, *the quicker the match finishes, the better* – so don't slow it down. Keep the tempo high. Some players speed up between points when they have the flow with them; this gives their opponent less chance to regroup mentally.

Try to collect as many points as possible. Momentum may well shift in time, and during the time it is with you, stay focussed and collect as many points as possible to add to your overall tally. Do not relax and think that you can afford to lose a few sloppy points because things are going your way. As any farmer will tell you, make hay while the sun shines!

Don't interrupt the match by arguing a line call too long, taking a towel break, or taking too long between points. Avoid interruptions when you have the momentum. In one match I watched, a player who was leading 21-12, 13-6 decided to stop and put a plaster on a minuscule cut on his elbow which was not even bleeding. This stoppage allowed his opponent to regroup and regain some momentum by perceiving the break as the start of the match again. This player effectively created a turning point against himself!

Make sure you are well prepared. Plan ahead before matches so that you can cope with anything that might frustrate you or cause a distraction. Make sure you have anything you might need with you: spare rackets (correctly strung), drinks, plasters, spare shoelaces, a change of shirt, sweatbands, energy bars, grips, grip powder, etc.

# Choking

A player choking is perhaps the best-known way for someone to create a turning point against themselves. Because it is perceived to be a mentally weak thing to do, if a player loses a lead through choking, they can then be affected mentally for the rest of the match. It can affect their self-esteem and may cause their performance to drop.

Players can choke for many different reasons and I am not going to try to cover them all here. There are many sports psychology explanations and different tools to deal with choking, ranging from relaxation techniques to positive imagery.

If you are an experienced badminton player, you undoubtedly know how tough it can be – on occasions – to close out a win. It's in no small part due to the scoring system (see later). It is only the non-experts who believe that losing a lead is a sign of weakness every time.

If choking starts to manifest when you are leading a match… there's no point in getting nervous. If your opponent is any good, they will be fighting harder and playing better at the end of the match, so you must always be prepared to work hard for another five minutes or more. How do you expect to win the last few points? Will any quality opponent tamely hit four shots into the net or out? Concentrate on your own game rather than relying on errors from your opponent.

Be prepared to work hard; nobody knows where the finish line might be. Even at match point, there is still work to be done. Be a badminton expert and be prepared to fight.

### Key points to remember when momentum is with you

- Put the radar on to make sure potential turning points against you are mere blips.
- It's not what goes wrong that matters; it's your reaction to it.
- Embrace the challenge.
- Keep control of your body language.
- Learn to deal with gamesmanship: choose the right battlefield.
- Keep the match running.
- Keep choking in perspective; be a badminton expert.

# 3. When momentum is in the balance

When things are *in the balance* – when the scales are waiting to be tipped by one player or the other – it can be an exciting or unnerving feeling. That's because, self-evidently, things could swing either way.

It exists when there is an equal matchup – in terms of standards – and can captivate an audience when both players are at their best and involved in an epic tussle. However, at other times, it can seem as if nothing much is happening, rather like two boxers sparring.

It can happen at the beginning of the match, but also occur well into the match, when neither player can find their rhythm and the game is full of errors from both individuals (such as when neither player is able to establish dominance on serve, or return of serve, or able to establish any penetration on their attack).

Whenever it occurs, though, it is the time when chances for surging ahead need to be created and taken.

You can tilt momentum in your favour by:

- Making clear decisions
- Grabbing it

- Being ready before you begin

- Coming back and going again!

## Make clear decisions

When things are in the balance and you want to gain momentum and break away from the opposition, you may be caught between thinking you are doing well (and thus wanting to maintain the status quo), versus being aware you need to break away (and therefore doing something different).

When things are in the balance, you need to make this decision: stick or twist?

It's a risk versus reward issue. We covered it earlier, and only you can make the decision based on the state of play and the opposition.

The important thing is to *stick with your decision*, and have confidence it will come good in the long run. If you don't make a decision, the opposition may well do so (see below).

## Don't wait… grab it

When the momentum is neutral, you may well be searching for answers, and may be caught between keeping the same tactics and making a change. This feeling can result in a lack of positive decision-making. The danger is that a player who hesitates in this situation is like a sprinter waiting on the line for their rival to shout "go". At this point, you should be looking to establish a flow of momentum in your favour. If you wait for your opponent to do something, it is possible that you will end up following the flow of momentum and raising your game too late. The saying *he who hesitates is lost* is very appropriate here.

You often hear of players *nearly* pulling off such an upset, then consoling themselves with the thought that there was nothing they could do when it came to it, because their opponent came up with the goods. Usually, this is because they waited for something to happen.

Higher-ranked players will often raise their game, spurred on by the realisation that they must act before it's too late. But how should you grab the momentum? What do you do to raise your game?

This has to depend partly on the journey of the match until this point, the type of opponent (see the 1*- 4* system later in the book) and the score at the time. If you have had the momentum with you – and things are now in the balance – it is a different feeling to having had momentum against you and the opponent has come back into the match. If the score is close, towards the end of the first game, and you are the favourite and being hunted, this may lead to one game of decisions. If neither of you are playing well, and both looking for a foothold at the start of the third game, this may lead to a different set of decisions.

A very good guide is to zone in on *specific tactics* you have discussed with your coach before the match. Plan your work and work your plan. Whatever you do, decide quickly, and commit to your decision. *Keep the future in your hands.*

## Be ready before you begin

Grasping the opportunity to surge ahead in the match can often mean being properly psyched-up to do so before the match begins.

This is particularly true if you are playing an opponent you are not expected to beat. You have to be mentally ready to take the opportunity when it comes along. Don't wait to see what happens; the opportunity will disappear quickly against the better players. (You can choose your phrase here from the following: *grasp the nettle, push them over the cliff,* or *take the bull by the horns*!)

A phrase we used with Anthony Clark, before playing matches against higher-ranked players, was *step up to the plate* (a baseball phrase). This came about after Anthony lost a number of matches to better and more experienced players early in his career, and seemed happy to have played well and pushed them close. Once he started 'stepping up to the plate' – believing in his strengths and realising his opportunities – Anthony became an exceptional world-class competitor.

## Come back and go

Grabbing the situation might simply mean urging yourself to forge ahead to win when you have pulled back from being well behind. Very often, you will see a player come back and draw level, only to relax and lose the game.

There are many examples of players who made a change in their game or renewed their efforts when they were behind, but as soon as they pulled level in the score, they thought the job was done and relaxed their fighting spirit. At the same time, the player in the lead might have been fearing their opponent drawing level, and when it happens, they relax because their fears have been realised. Sometimes, this releases tension; sometimes, it makes them angry. Either way, their energy and fighting spirit often goes up.

This change in energy on court from either one or both players is why the momentum can switch again, and the player who has come back can lose. So, if you are the player who fights to draw level, be determined to *keep fighting* and surge ahead. Be aware that the period when the scores are level is key if you intend to win. Never draw level and wait to see what happens – **come back and go!**

**Key points to remember when momentum is in the balance**

- Make clear decisions

- Grab the momentum before the opposition does

- Be ready before you begin by being well prepared

- Come back and go!

# 4. When momentum is against you

When the flow of the match is against you, it can be frustrating. This is particularly true if things are against you because you haven't played that well. Your opponent may seem to be playing with increased energy and confidence, and key points seem to go against you. Things that normally work, or which maybe worked earlier on in the match, now just keep narrowly failing. If luck plays its part, it doesn't seem to be in your favour. Small things that don't irritate you when you have the momentum with you are now distractions. It can feel like you are swimming against the tide.

However, you are not alone! All players experience these feelings.

At such moments, it is easy to feel that things are slipping away and to become frustrated. Your body language may begin to tell the story of your feelings and may give even more encouragement to your opponent. How best do you deal with this situation?

Your aim during this phase is to regain momentum. This can be done in a variety of ways, and here are some suggestions – based on real-world player feedback – when people feel that momentum is against them:

## Reframe it

Sometimes, you need to see things differently. As Einstein once said, "In the middle of difficulty lies opportunity". If you always see the bright side of a situation, it can make a big difference. Here are two examples of reframing a seemingly negative situation:

# Reframe it – Anthony Clark

At a regional/East Midlands Under-15 training camp in Paris, at The National Institute of Sport, one of our players – Anthony Clark (who went on to be a Commonwealth and European champion and two times World silver medallist) – was locked into a frustrating battle with the French number 1 junior.

*A young Anthony Clark.*

It was a match that Anthony felt he should win comfortably, but he was noticeably struggling.

He had won the first set with relative ease and had a strong lead in the second set before his opponent pegged him back and overtook him to lead 17-11. To make matters worse, Anthony had broken the last of his favourite rackets, and his world was falling apart. To be honest, as a coach in the chair courtside, I was as frustrated as Anthony was, watching him tear himself apart and feeling completely helpless to support him; everything I tried to suggest appeared to have a worsening effect.

Inevitably, Anthony lost the second game and – in the interval before the deciding third set after listening to all of Anthony's negativity and problems – I simply said in frustration, "For goodness sake, you could beat this guy playing with a frying pan if you had to."

Apparently, after the match, Anthony said that all he thought about after that interval was playing with a frying pan and simply getting the shuttle over the net one more time than his opponent. He went on to win the third game comfortably.

He had forgotten the fact that, as a younger kid, he had thrived on putting his neck on the block and proving he could beat people (for example, playing cricket with a broomstick as a bat). He had allowed himself to become completely overwhelmed by the journey of the match and the situation he found himself in.

Whatever the situation, it's rarely as bad as it seems when you take the emotion out of it and reframe matters. Imagine you are 21-16, 18-10 up, and your opponent comes back to 18-17. With only seconds in-between points, you may not get your mental approach right to renew your energy. But imagine you were able to travel back in time – to before the match began – and someone offered you 21-16 18-17 as a scoreline to *start the match with*, instead of 0-0, and gave you two hours to get ready. You would surely arrive ready to play. Well, we haven't discovered time travel yet, but you can get the same attitude simply by learning to renew efforts quicker.

## Don't rush

If the momentum is with you, the quicker the match finishes, the better. It follows that when the momentum is against you, the longer you are on court, the better. So, it is vital you take your time between points and don't allow yourself to be rushed.

This is sometimes not so easy to do. The natural reaction to having things go against you, is to want to make them right *quickly*. However, rushing when you have things going against you – and you are feeling in turmoil inside – can only lead to more errors. The same one-off quick 'wonder winners' that hit the line when things go for you, are the ones that miss the line when you're up against it.

## Body language

Even if you don't feel great, keep a check that your body language isn't giving you away.

In wars, planes fly over the enemy dropping leaflets telling them bad news, such as their supplies are running out, their superiors have not told them that many of their soldiers have surrendered, that they should give up now before they are killed. Badminton is not war, but you should certainly not be letting your opponent know when you're not feeling as good as you would like!

And don't get too focussed on yourself. Watch the body language of your opponent and remember to keep doing it. If you were a boxer, this would be easy, because you are only a few feet away; in badminton, you have to look closely and regularly if you want to pick up any signals. Turning points can occur in the mind of your opponent. Who knows, they may be carrying an injury, may be worried that they will lose a lead because they regularly do, or may not be happy with the tension of a new racket. You may not know what causes turning points, but you should be able to sense them if you keep an eye on your opponent's body language.

## Switch on the radar

Keep on a constant lookout for potential turning points for you.

## Radar Down – Example

A player I coach was once losing an international match. She was 11-16, and the momentum was against her, but only just. The match was very close, with each point tightly contested and my player was losing only because her opponent was hitting a few one-off winners. But, crucially, my player was reading the score rather than the match and, as a consequence, was feeling quite demoralised.

Perhaps because she was feeling low, she failed to seize two opportunities that were created for turning the momentum her way. One was a drop-dead net cord winner after a 40-shot rally; the other a brilliant deceptive cross-court shot she played from an almost impossible position.

While not registering the significance of the points she won, she had nonetheless managed to get herself back to 17-18 down when another golden opportunity presented itself. She again failed to spot it. An official came on to the court to assist with an electronic scoreboard error. She could have used this distraction to her advantage by realising the potential opportunity for her opponent to become anxious about her lead being eroded. Yet my player became more irritated and upset by the disruption than her opponent and lost an opportunity to bring about a swing in momentum in her favour.

You should welcome outside distractions – the more, the better. If you keep your cool, they represent opportunities for **your opponent** to be distracted!

*"I learned to welcome distractions on the court, to use them
as a weapon against my opponent – to handle them better than
them, and gain a performance edge." Peter Gade*

## How to create turning points in your favour

As well as keeping the radar on, and being able to spot potential turning points, you
should try to *create* turning points. There are different ways you can help to create turning
points in your favour through your own actions:

- Changing tactics

- Not changing tactics

- Spotting patterns of play

- Capitalising on potential turning points

## Changing tactics

You could consider changing tactics. Chapter Six looks at tactical choices in more detail, but for now, here is one example of how changing tactics can turn a match around.

# Don't Be Afraid of Change

In my younger days, I played an international junior tournament in Belgium. It was one of my first ever international trips, and none of us knew much about any of our opponents at that stage.

I was being hosted by the head coach of a Belgian club and his family, who knew a lot about the young Belgium players. He offered me some tactical advice before going into the match as my opponent played for a rival club.

He told me that he was very attacking and liked to play short points, hitting winning shots early on in the rally. The coach told me that I should play long, consistent rallies and wear my opponent down until he made a mistake.

At the match – and from the outset – my opponent was all over me; he had so much time and could hit winners with ease from all areas of the court. He was completely controlling the match, winning the first set 15-6 (15 point scoring system) and leading 8-2 in the second set.

Almost out of desperation, I decided to try to put the shuttle on the floor before he did, as he had been doing so rather a lot.

In taking this approach, I took on a sense of urgency, increased my intensity, and took his 'time' away from him. I made him play on the defensive, where he was nowhere near as good. I clawed my way back into the match and eventually had a comfortable third-set victory.

It wasn't until later that evening that I fully understood what had happened, and that I had managed to change tactics in order to create change.

## Not changing tactics

Sometimes, you may not need to change tactics, but simply do what you are doing *better*, or allow time for things to have their effect.

You should always begin by trying to improve your existing tactics.

You may be dominating the points every time you achieve a great length to the back of the court, but be missing long – out the back – too often. You may also have worked very good openings but just missed the final 'kill', which has tilted things against you. The answer – in this case – would be to continue, but to get better length and to capitalise on the 'kill' opportunities you have created.

If you are playing good consistent badminton but have lost a close first game, you may not need to change either. Consistent, controlled play that maintains a level, sometimes takes time to have its effect on the opponent. The effect is like that of an arm wrestle. If you keep the pressure on for long enough, then the opponent will wilt. Some wilt sooner, and others take longer, depending on how mentally tough they are.

## Spotting patterns of play

Knowing the likely patterns of your opponent can help create a turning point in your favour. You can scout your opponent to note their favourite patterns, or you can simply observe carefully and gather information as the match goes on.

For example, a player may always smash straight, or always kill into the gap, or serve to the 'T' as opposed to the body or out wide. If you make a mental note of these patterns, it allows you to make a best guess at a crucial time later in the match.

If you snatch the type of point that your opponent had been winning (e.g., them committing to an easy kill on the forecourt) on a big point, this could create a turning point in your favour.

This is why in many Asian countries – originally Korea and China – players practise intensely on reactive defence and returning the shuttle back over the net somehow, rescuing lost causes in the hope of capitalising upon their opponent's disbelief.

*Japanese Men's Doubles – refuse to let the shuttle land on their side of the court.*

Asian doubles pairs, and particularly Chinese mixed doubles pairs, have developed an expertise in recovering from seemingly impossible situations by somehow returning the shuttle when their opponents appear to have an easy kill. Their skills at reactive, desperate, hustle defence are extremely refined as they are fully aware of the benefits it can have to themselves and the emotional damage it can have on their opposition. I believe – on occasion – but especially in the mixed doubles, they purposely set this situation up, tempting the female opponent to commit and go for the kill, which then leaves gaps on the court to be exploited by their reactive, desperation defence.

With this knowledge in mind, you will often see Korean and Chinese players setting up multi-feed exercises where they aggressively bury their 'finishing off' opportunities into the ground. Currently, you will also find a few top players that seem to wait until very close to the end of the match, at critical points, before revealing their extremely effective and unexpected drive serve, taking everybody by surprise, including the service judges. You had better be mindful of this threat and be ready to utilise it in your favour.

# The Wobbler – Change Things Up!

The mixed doubles final in the Denmark Open 2006 in Aarhus was the scene of another remarkable moment where a split-second of genius – a courageous shot selection at a critical moment by a player – won the match and the title. The immediate reaction of their opponents and the crowd, however, could so easily have influenced the umpire and court officials to respond differently.

Anthony Clark and Donna Kellogg of England were up against Danish favourites and reigning champions Thomas Layburn and Kamilla Juhl in the final. Thomas and Kamilla had the incredible backing of the full Danish crowd behind them and were utilising this to establish their authority, cruising to a comfortable first set victory of 21-14. Anthony and Donna were fighting hard and somehow managed to stay in contention showing extreme resilience, as they did at so many times throughout their careers. They levelled the match at one set all and, in doing so, quietened down the crowd ever so slightly for a short period.

Here they were, locked in battle at 20-20 in the deciding game, with the Danish crowd doing everything in their power to get their Danish countrymen over the line to victory. They managed to get themselves to match point at 22-21, and the crowd went deathly silent.

What happened next is forever etched in my mind and appeared to all happen in super slow motion. Incredibly bravely, Donna used the 'Wobbler' and hit the best serve I have ever seen to completely ace Thomas Layburn; she drove her drive serve up the middle line of the service box without him even moving.

The service judge was silent. The umpire announced "Game" and then "Match" – Anthony and Donna immediately raised their arms in delight and then froze. There was a moment of eerie silence that swept through the whole arena, broken by Thomas who smashed his racket violently into the ground in protest. Kamilla, on seeing this, did exactly the same but even more violently. The crowd finally reacted thunderously in support of Thomas and Kamilla, believing they had been duped by the officials and that Donna may have broken the service laws (which, of course, she had not; she had simply shown them something different at a critical moment).

In amongst all the frenzy and madness, Anthony and Donna appeared to be frozen to the spot in the middle of the court, not quite knowing how to react. In my coach's chair at the side of the court, I could sense that there might be enough chaos and noise to intimidate the umpire into reversing her decision – I only just managed to make my anxious shout heard to Donna and Anthony over the riotous crowd. "Shake the Umpire's hand, grab your bags, and get outta there FAST!"

They snapped into realisation and into gear immediately – it then became the fastest exit from a court in a final that I've ever seen! They had won the title fairly and squarely with a moment of genius from Donna. There should be no way that this reaction and the influence of the crowd should take that away from the English pair, even though you could sense that was exactly what was about to happen.

The "Wobbler' is a variation of a serve that Donna used to throw in very, very occasionally. Perhaps once in a whole tournament (if at all) with the intention of totally surprising her opponent and showing them something completely different. Perhaps creating a turning point and therefore affecting momentum.

It is a risky strategy and something that is very hard to deliver consistently. Basically, you set up and prepare, ready to deliver your service as normal. With your feet planted securely, just as you are about to take the racket back to address the shuttle – you slowly move the racket and shuttle horizontally approximately 30 cms to the left or right, giving your opponent a completely different angle to cover. You almost move it to the point where you are close to losing your balance, as you are unable to move your feet before striking the shuttle – hence the process acquiring the name "Wobbler" from our team.

## Reacting to positive potential turning points

When a potential turning point happens in your favour, you should allow it to give you a boost and show this in your body language. Your opponent might not have recognised it as a potential turning point and extra energy from you can introduce doubt into their mind.

You will often see an experienced player visibly pick up in their energy level when this happens. They will be livelier in their routine before the point starts, they may call out the score with more confidence in their voice, and even shout "come on" to themselves.

Players who have had momentum turn suddenly against them before, may start to worry when they see your reaction. Again, don't forget that the bigger the swing in energy – at times like this – the bigger the swing in momentum.

GB Olympic medallist Gail Emms was once asked, "What do you not want to see when momentum is against you?" Her answer, "I certainly don't want to see my opponents up at the net, and looking at me whilst screaming in delight!"

*Spanish World Champion Carolina Marin always displays*
*an immense amount of energy and positivity both*
*within the rallies and in-between points.*

## Fair play

Never attempt to create turning points by bending the rules. The enjoyment of winning is very closely linked to the enjoyment of overcoming obstacles over the journey towards victory. Don't let that journey be tainted by gamesmanship. Keep your badminton on the badminton battlefield.

## Key points to remember when momentum is against you:

- Show fighting spirit.
- Don't rush.
- Keep a check on your body language.
- Switch on the radar.

- Keep an eye on your opponent.

- Spot potential turning points quickly by having a positive attitude.

- Maintain a lead by using your imagination.

- Review your tactics.

- Spot patterns of play.

- Be aware of gamesmanship tactics.

# 5. When momentum is totally against you

When the momentum is totally against you, it is the easiest thing in the world to believe it's just not your day. If you are, for example, 16-10 down in the third game, having been a game up, it can seem that it's too big a hill to climb to turn things around, and that the flow of the match is strongly with your opponent. It's at times like these that you might wonder why you bother playing at all! It is also easy to display negative body language, thus giving your opponent even more encouragement.

The fact is, however, that matches do turn around regularly from seemingly impossible positions. You are only in a *stage of momentum*, and if you can get out of it to the next level, then turning points become more possible and the nerves of your opponent may work in your favour. If you are to make a comeback, this bit is the most difficult. Moving up a stage when you are well behind is mentally tougher than moving up a stage at any other time.

Danish legend Peter Gade once said, "I enjoy the game so much more when I have momentum. I see solutions and not limitations. It demands so much more energy and power from me when it is against me."

## Don't lose hope

The most important thing when the momentum is totally against you is not to lose hope. It is not easily done, because your opponent is full of confidence, has the cushion of a lead, and is trying to finish you off. That would be tough enough at any time, but it usually happens when you are probably feeling frustrated, disheartened, and maybe tired – having spent time and energy getting yourself into this unfavourable position!

Your opponent may seem to be playing too well for you to have a chance of victory, but you should remember how easy it is to play well when the momentum is totally with you. It is the same for them. They won't be as good when the momentum has shifted.

The road to making a comeback is steep, at first, but it will get easier if you can dig in and get a foothold. Once you have stuck in and begun to make a comeback, two factors will work in your favour: you will begin to feel better, and your opponent will dislike the fact that it's not as easy as it was. This double change in energy gives the best conditions for a change in the flow of the match.

# Athens 2004 Olympic Mixed Doubles Final - Robertson/Emms [GBR] v Zhang Jun/GAO Ling [CHN]

An example from Andy Wood

It was the Olympic Mixed Doubles final in Athens 2004. It was the end of the first game, and I rushed out of the allocated coach's chair to meet Nathan Robertson and Gail Emms courtside for the coaching interval as they trundled off the court in forlorn despair.

Here they were – fulfilling a lifetime ambition and creating history by competing in an Olympic final. Having played the best badminton of their lives in the preceding days to reach the final, they had captured the imagination of our nation and commanded amazing British support in the crowd and around the world for this final. However, they had just been decimated by the most ferocious, aggressive, and intimidating performance I had ever witnessed in the first game, and in doing so, only managed to accrue one single point! The first emotion to overcome was 'shellshock'!

Having had the opportunity to take a breath, my job was to help re-establish belief to get over the shellshock and realise this match was still alive and they could still win by starting again and winning the next two games. With a quick review of the tactics and a good start, they began to claw their way back into the match and shift momentum.

The insanely powerful smashes from Zhang Jun started to be returned, and returned with interest. The speed at which Gao Ling was controlling the forecourt started to be matched by Gail Emms and then superseded. The belief returned and that confidence gain was visibly transmitted to the crowd who came alive in an incredibly powerful way as they too believed, or dared to dream. Robertson and Emms levelled the match at one game all with an outstanding and courageous second game performance. The deciding game was an intensely contested affair, swinging back and forth with both pairs gaining slight advantages at certain times. Sadly, it was not to be for the British pair as they were edged out in an exceptionally close finish with some incredibly exciting badminton being exhibited by both pairs. Robertson and Emms had to be content with the first ever Silver Olympic medal in badminton for Great Britain, but it could so easily have been more.

Nonetheless, how Nathan and Gail managed to find a way to get back into that match was nothing short of remarkable, considering the formidable supremacy of their opponents and the amount of momentum against them.

*Nathan Robertson and Gail Emms on the podium*
*with their Silver medals at Athens Olympics 2004.*

## Take your time and play one point at a time

When the momentum is totally against you, take your time. Slow things down and find some way of getting points on the scoreboard whilst letting the steam go out of your opponent's game. Momentum in this situation tends to change slowly (the creeping change mentioned earlier), and you have to build the foundations for a change.

> "I think stopping momentum and changing momentum are different things because you can stop it by breaking it up, and then that would be the start of actually trying to change it round into your favour. So, I don't think it just switches. I think it sometimes needs to be stopped before you can consider changing it in your favour."
>
> Nathan Robertson

Playing one point at a time is very important. When you are well behind in momentum, it is not possible just to collect points quickly like you can when you are in the lead. It's a bit like trying to get out of a hole. Put great emphasis on the very next point.

One point can make all the difference. If you can stay in touch with your opponent on the scoreboard – when you are well behind in momentum – you will be closer for when things turn around. For example, if you can somehow stay 3 or 4 points behind your opponent when you change at 11-6 down in the third when your opponent starts to wobble, or you start to build some momentum.

China as a badminton nation are such masters of attaining multi-point runs that we – the GB Badminton team – adopted a 3-point rule. If you lost two consecutive points, that set an alarm; if it got to 3 points then that meant you had to take time, reset, and change your thinking to halt the slide. The aim of the rule was to provide a process to ensure you were not the victim of their multi-point flow – an easy trap to fall into.

This is where the phrase *weathering the storm* applies. You hear it in other sports as well. In football, in this situation, getting the ball and somehow keeping possession of it is crucial. The same applies in badminton – you have to find a way of staying in the match. Staying in the match is the best way of building foundations for a change in the future (e.g., a potential turning point that occurs when you are not so far behind in the momentum).

It is particularly important not to lose hope when you are *tired*. You never know how tired your opponent is as well. Don't let things slide. Stay in touch with the score by trying to win the next point and taking each point one at a time.

## Have a cunning plan

Here's an interesting ploy. If you are a game up, but well behind in the *second* game of a three-set match, you might consider the effect of starting the final set fresh. In other words, take a break from the tactics and intensity of play that won you the first set by deliberately playing *exhibition badminton*, as if to create the impression that you are no longer trying or no longer care about the outcome of the match. The plan is twofold and – in a sense – is a win-win ploy.

If you lose the second game, you lull your opponent into a sense of false security; for the crucial start of the third set, you can hit them with different tactics and/or a new attitude. However, this approach of exhibition badminton may also allow you to unsettle your opponent with quick, spectacular *one-off* winners to get yourself quickly out of *the momentum totally against you* stage. It is then

*Taufik Hidiyat.*

possible to revert to the strategy that won you the first set, knowing that you have got back the necessary momentum and that your opponent's nerves may become a factor as you continue your comeback.

It is important to think carefully before you employ this tactic as it can derail you too. It is certainly risky and you should have knowledge of your own capabilities to switch on and switch off. Some competitors are certainly masters of this approach; for example, Lin Dan (two-time Olympic champion, five-time world champion), as well as Indonesian legend Taufik Hidiyat.

## Read the future

Momentum moves through the five stages outlined above, and sometimes you cannot control it. Therefore, be wise and understand there is a strong chance that it may change. Let that knowledge give you hope when you are well behind, and keep you alert to dangers when you are well in front.

The key to responding best to the ebbs and flow of momentum is to control your *own* mental stability, and watch for signs of your opponent's change in mental state, particularly after obviously significant events.

Remember, the most common reasons for momentum to change:

- A change in your opponent's mental state – either gradual or sudden.
- A change in your mental state – either gradual or sudden.
- A change in your tactics.
- A change in your opponent's tactics.

## Look at your own game

The best players are those who are equally tough in all stages of momentum. What would it take to turn yourself into a player who is excellent in any of the five situations? Which of the five situations are you weak in, and why?

The possibilities for a player being poor in a given stage are endless, so we will avoid giving too many examples. But be honest with yourself and identify areas for improvement. Then, ask your coach to help or maybe even a sports psychologist. They have a whole array of mental tools for improving certain areas – from correct performance goal setting, to in-between point routines, imagery, relaxation techniques and focus control. There are plenty of techniques (most of which are easy to understand and use) that can help you improve your own individual momentum on court.

## Key points to remember when momentum is totally against you

- Don't lose hope.
- Take your time.
- Have a cunning plan.
- Read the future.
- Look at your own game.

# Chapter 5: Developing Your Game

We have covered different options for dealing with each stage of momentum, and we have also highlighted some of the opportunities and dangers that can occur at different scorelines. Now, armed with this information, you will be better informed about what is to come in matches, and better able to deal with twists, turns, and significant events. It is also important to remember that all competitors are in the same boat; do not think that *your* feelings and challenges are unique to you.

But now, we can take this information further and use your knowledge of how matches progress (and the type of challenges that regularly occur) to take advantage and develop two things.

1. The ability to respond effectively to match events.

2. The ability to assess the state of play using 'big picture' thinking.

> "In transitioning from junior to senior international badminton, I was very lucky to play with experienced partners. I quickly learnt that navigating my way through the twists and turns of a match and responding optimally gave me another weapon and a decisive advantage over my opponent."
>
> Nathan Robertson

Having an awareness as to the 'state of play' – so you know *where* you are in the match, and where you have come from – is like having a compass and a map that can be applied to any match, no matter how idiosyncratic.

If you learn to stand back from the match, and quickly assess the state of play, you are much better placed to decide on the best way forward. Players who do this can adapt their games based on the situation in front of them; they can change the direction of the match in their favour.

In turn, recognising significant (and potentially significant) match events, and respond effectively to them, is a real skill. It doesn't matter how you achieve it, it's simply whether you are able to respond quickly and effectively to whatever happens.

Players who respond effectively and regain their competitiveness quickly after a setback might do so because they are annoyed and get fired up to right a perceived wrong, or because they are calm and quickly accept the situation to focus on the process. The result is the same… their performance doesn't drop for long, if it drops at all.

Developing these two skills doesn't happen overnight, and takes regular competition and reflection on matches played. Learning from match to match is at the heart of improving, and this is done by contemplating previous matches; a process that informs planning for future matches.

*PV Sindhu, always totally aware of the state of play.*

# 1. Assessing the state of play

When should you assess the state of play?

During the match – in the heat of the battle – your focus should be on the task at hand; you should be in the moment, in the here and now. This ability to zoom in on what's important is key, but this zoomed in approach, alone, is not enough.

Imagine rowing a boat across an ocean to an island. You're rowing with fantastic focus on each stroke of the oar, totally in the moment, and with maximum motivation and effort, but not taking into account the tidal currents and when they changed. You could be rowing the best you have ever rowed... in the wrong direction!

The more experienced you become, the quicker you can assess the state of the game. Because the skill becomes almost second nature, you can read where the game could go next as events occur. It's similar to your awareness of the weather outside right now. You're not focussing on it, or making a checklist to go through it, but your awareness guides what clothes you'll wear and whether to turn the heating or air conditioning up or down.

Assessing the state of play is the same as 'zooming out' and even the most experienced players take time to do this. They mentally stand back from the match and take a wider view to check (and perhaps adjust) their approach.

Whether you are already very experienced or are learning the skill of making decisions based on the state of play, it is important to identify the right times to stand back and think about the state of play and the direction of the match.

Do not do this when you are immersed in the game. Instead, use:

- End of sets
- Mid-game breaks
- Court repair or mopping
- Injury timeouts

## How do you make decisions based on the state of play?

When making in-match decisions, deciding where to start and which solution applies to which problem is not easy. Is the best approach to impose your game or to stop the opposition from playing theirs effectively? Should you focus on being in the here and now (using breathing exercises), or should you raise your energy and attack more?

This is a common problem, and it's the same with all challenges. Take exams in school, for example. Learners learn theories in blocks, but exam questions don't come in blocks and don't tell you which of the possible solutions you should apply. At the start of the maths question, it does not say, "This question can be answered using Pythagoras Theorem".

It's the same in matches; you have to work things out for yourself. However, we can offer a thought *process* that has been proven to help players' thinking.

During a match, you want to keep your strategic thinking top line, and simply ask yourself three basic questions:

1. What is the current state of play?

2. *What* do I want to do?

3. *How* do I want to do it?

Let's look in more detail at each of these and establish some supplementary questions.

## 1. What is the current state of play?

To assess the state of play, you need to consider the scoreline, who has the momentum, and why.

The score gives the context and therefore guides decision making. For example, having the momentum but being behind in the score is different from having momentum and being ahead in the score.

Deciding who has the momentum at the time means assessing the factors that are influencing the direction of the match. This can include the change in score, body language, decision-making, and performance gaps between players. It may be that no side has any meaningful momentum.

This question relates to the balance of the match at any given point. Other ways of putting it are:

- 'Who is on top?'

- 'Who is in the ascendancy?'

- 'Who has the upper hand?'

The skill is to observe what is happening from another person's point of view, perhaps as if watching the match from the stands. It may involve managing your emotions, so you make rational judgements, not emotional ones.

You might want to ask yourself what your coach, or a fellow competitor, would say if they were watching. Or you could imagine you are a gambler who has decided to bet all their money on your opponent! What aspects of their game, and the game right now, would make you feel confident? What aspects of their game would make you feel concerned?

Feeding into this analysis is an assessment of the journey of the match to this point (including how the score has developed, who previously had momentum and match events), your own current performance, and the match up with the opposition. A useful supplementary question to ask is, '*How* did we get here?'. Thinking about the journey of the match to this point allows you to fathom how likely it is that the current state of play will change or not.

For example, if momentum is against you due to a series of lucky, one-off, unrepeatable events in favour of the opposition, and there is still enough of the match to go, you may stay assured that you should continue as you are (perhaps adjusting to remain especially patient and calm). On the other hand, if momentum is against you because of a specific tactic the opposition are employing, and which has taken you by surprise, a countermeasure may well be required. And that means a change in the game plan.

One other useful skill is being able to see things through the eyes of the opposition. How are *they* seeing the game now? What are *they* prepared for? What are *they* not prepared for? What are *they* hoping you will do? What are *they* hoping you will not do?

## 2. What do I want to do?

Having assessed the state of play – and decided if momentum is for you, against you, or in the balance – and taken the current scoreline into account, this leads you to consider whether the aim is:

- To gain momentum
- To maintain momentum
- To regain momentum

This may seem obvious, but you will probably have some decisions to make. For example, if you have the momentum, do you wish to attempt to gain *more* momentum and extend your lead, or stick with what you have and manage the game until the conclusion? If you are looking to regain momentum, do you need to kill their momentum first by letting the steam go out of the game, or do you want to switch to a much more aggressive approach?

## 3. How do I want to do this?

We know from earlier that the two performance factors you can consciously change are tactical and mental.

## Tactical Changes

The first step to making logical decisions in matches is understanding what your *repeatable patterns* are (see above), and what you do when you vary from them. Likewise, you can make tactical changes if you understand your opponents and know *their repeatable patterns*.

Rexy Mainaky of Indonesia was an expert in this approach, and appeared to know exactly what an opposition's next shot was likely to be.

# Reading the Game

### An example from Andy Wood

Rexy Mainaky of Indonesia, former Olympic Men's Doubles Champion, worked with us at the National Badminton Centre, for our Olympic preparation for the 2004 Olympic Games in Athens.

Although he had retired as a player by this time, he regularly competed and interacted in practice with our Olympic Doubles Squad. Within days of his arrival, it felt like he had completely worked out all of our players' strengths, weaknesses, and repeatable patterns, simply by spending time amongst them in matchplay.

He seemed to be able to read exactly where they were going to hit the shuttle in any given situation.

This ability that Rexy had, created such joy and inspiration in the training hall; he was a great source of motivation for the players.

*Rexy Mainaky coaching how to use your head.*

One example of tactical decision making might be when you are 17-17 in the deciding game and your opponent is nervous. Here, sticking to your familiar repeatable patterns and avoiding new, riskier patterns may be advisable to maintain your consistency and keep the opposition playing when they are less likely to execute well.

However, imagine you had held a big lead in the second, having won the first game, and you were now struggling to stay with your opponent in the third. Trying to create 'change' against the flow (or run of play) may well demand coming up with something different – which might mean a one-off variation (or several) to snatch the momentum back.

On the other hand, if you were well down and have come back to win the set by playing one-off badminton – because you had nothing to lose – then at the start of the next set, you may need to return to repeatable patterns. You may not be able to rely on a rich vein of one-off badminton now the 'nothing to lose' feeling has gone.

At the change of ends, you can reflect how the points are being won and lost, keeping track of the repeatable patterns versus the one-off events. This will help you keep some perspective on what the score is telling you. If you have lost a close set, but missed a few one-offs you shouldn't have attempted, while your opponent has made some they wouldn't normally make, then you could have cause to be optimistic. If the reverse is true, you shouldn't rest on your laurels.

> Repeatable patterns of play are a sequence of shots that players use regularly, often because they are confident and comfortable with them.
>
> They even may be unaware of their habits.

The person who controls the *repeatable patterns* in a match very often dictates with whom the underlying momentum lies. Seeing who controls the tactical patterns of a match can sometimes be done more easily from a distance.

For example, watching a junior match from a distance, you may see the scoreboard at 8-11 in the first game, and perhaps notice the mother of the girl who was losing, looking very tense, and pacing the balcony above the court. However, from a distance, you might also be able to tell that she actually has nothing to worry about, because her daughter is playing aggressively and moving well, is calmer, and is continually creating opportunities she is just missing. Her daughter's opponent, on the other hand, is stressed, making impressive shots she can't keep on making, and is benefiting from a few lucky net chords. In other words, her daughter is controlling the repeatable patterns. This was, in fact, a real example where the first player went on to win 21-16, 21-15.

Being able to analyse who is controlling the repeatable patterns like this can also help you mentally. It is important not to panic if things don't go your way immediately. If you know you are controlling the repeatable patterns, you can stay calm. If you just react to the score, panic, and rush to hit winners to get back into the match, you are more likely to lose momentum quickly.

**Task**

*When you are next watching a match, try asking yourself, "If the same repeatable tactical patterns that have happened so far keep happening, who will win?"*

*Choosing one player, would you advise a change in their tactics? A slight adaptation? Or to stay with what they're doing but improve execution?*

**Mental Changes**

Are you currently in the best mental state to execute the above tasks? A simple way of reviewing your mental approach – in light of the state of play – is to use the common reflection tool stop/start/continue. Namely:

- What do you want to stop doing?

- What do you want to start doing?

- What do you want to continue doing?

## Making a decision

The final and most important aspect is to prioritise your thoughts and make a decision.

Taking decisions is not always easy as there are consequences to these decisions, whether in a badminton match or life in general. All decisions contain an element of risk, so when considering your options, you should also determine how much risk is involved with each option before prioritising them and making your decision.

In some situations, you may decide you can't afford to take a risk to change dramatically. In other situations (e.g., losing heavily), you may be more adventurous because you can't afford not to take a risk, as you have nothing to lose given what's happening.

Ask yourself the questions:

- 'What are my options?'

- 'What is important now?'

It may be more than one thing, but it's best not to have more than one or two simple actions. In the heat of the battle, you don't want to overthink things!

It's also important to *commit* to your decision to give yourself the best chance of executing the tasks. You can review everything later on, and learn from them.

## Pre-planned decisions:

You may have already worked through some 'what if' scenarios for each of the above, and have some pre-prepared plans to employ.

If so, great. If not, work up some pre-prepared plans by going through the different scenarios below.

## State of Play Scenario:

Let's look at a specific match scenario, and think through the three questions that will help develop your game intelligence:

- What is the state of play?

- What do you want to do?

- How do you want to do it?

We'll use the example of maintaining momentum.

You have worked hard in the final set and now lead 16-11 with momentum for you. However, the opposition have not given up, and there is still work to be done to get over the finish line.

Two players with a similar style may take a very different approach to maintaining momentum. Player 1 takes the view that when you have the momentum and have moved ahead in the scoreline, you have something you don't want to lose whilst the opposition is feeling frustrated. "I will adjust my game by tightening it to *reduce errors* and make the opposition feel like they have a hill to climb. I will make them aware it's going to take a big effort to get back into the match at a time when they aren't feeling great. The last thing I want is to take any risks and let them back into the match quickly and easily."

Player 2, on the other hand, (in exactly the same situation), takes the view that they now have a cushion (in terms of lead) and want to take advantage of it by stepping up a gear. They look to play faster and more aggressively. "I want them to feel that I am much better than they are by using the freedom of having the momentum to use more variety, take a few more risks, perhaps play more to their strengths and beat them at their game whilst I'm feeling good. I know that if they do come back, I can always return to the tactics that gained me the momentum. It keeps them guessing as they don't know which is my real game."

Both are very successful players, and we couldn't argue one approach is better than the other. There are advantages and disadvantages to each approach.

What we can say, though, is that both players are assessing the state of play and making adjustments to their game in order to maintain and hopefully build more momentum in their favour. They do this to win the match as efficiently as possible.

Take a moment to consider what you would do in this situation? Consider how you might adjust either your tactical or mental approach, if at all. There is no right or wrong answer, only *what works for you*.

# 2. Responding to match events

This can be done by working through some what-if scenarios (although given what we know about matches, they are more 'what-when' than 'what-if'), and can also be done by examining your in-game match responses and reviewing them.

Think about how you would respond to the following scenarios:

- You lose the first game 19-21, win the second 21-12 and – having generally regained control of the match – suddenly, at 4-4 in the third, you miss your favourite, most consistent shot in the next three consecutive rallies to go 4-7 down.

- At 20-18 up, your opponent makes two very questionable line calls on your shots, calling them out when you are sure they were in, bringing the score back to 20 all.

- You save three match points from 16-20 behind in the deciding game – when you were feeling down and out – and bring the score back to 19-20.

- You won the first game 21-14, and just thought you had won the second game and match when winning the rally whilst serving at 20-18 up. Your opponent refuses to shake hands, stating that the score had not been 20-18 but 18 all – the referee comes onto court, and after a long delay, rules that you must restart from 18 all.

- At 14-18 down, your opponent serves into the net, and then returns serve into the net for the first time in the match, to bring the score to 16-18 down.

- You were 20-17 up and playing great, but have just failed to convert two set points to make the score 20-19. You are feeling tight, and your opposition is getting in your face with aggressive body language.

Which of these situations do you feel you need to improve? You may wish to focus on one or two of these examples, or you may wish to come up with an example from your own experience in recent matches.

And now consider the following questions:

- Do you think you could deal with this situation in an effective way?
- How would you *feel* in this situation?
- What would you be thinking?
- How do you think you should respond?
- Which tools might help you to do this? (See our Tactical/Mental options list in the next chapter.)

Of course, the above situations are very specific, and our aim here is not to help you prepare for such *exact* examples! The aim is to help you think about the types of common challenges players face in a game and help you get prepared for them.

# In-match responses

Let's now turn our attention to what happens once you're in the match. The first step is to recognise what the match events are, and review your responses to them. You may be able to do this by reflecting on recent matches, or you may wish – in the first instance – to use the sheet below (following your next few matches) to learn more.

When thinking about your response, we know that both tactical and mental factors are the areas to focus on. However, it is often a combination of both; your response involves a tactical task to be executed, with your mental skills supporting you to do this effectively.

Without effective mental skills (trained or untrained), executing your desired tactics may be more difficult. For example, it's hard to make decisions with clarity if you are over-emotional; it's hard to execute a skill when distracted; it's hard to execute a skill when feeling anxious; it's hard to stick to a task when disheartened.

Mental toughness is hard to measure because what happens inside a player's head is invisible to those observing. But what you can see is a player's response. Therefore, one way to judge how effective the response is, though, is to see how long it takes you to resume your best level of competitiveness, based on how it looks to the opposition through your body language and in-play decision making.

An example of a lightning-quick assessment of a situation, and an effective response, follows.

# Mike Tredgett – Rapid Response

An example from Andy Wood

In the very same match example that we mentioned earlier ('Maximising Home Court Advantage'), where one stand was left empty and the home crowd effectively established a visual blind by moving stands after each game, another strange and memorable event occurred.

As a young, inexperienced competitor at this level, I was extremely nervous to be playing at all, but also to be partnering a former legend of British Badminton... Mike Tredgett (former World Champion, All England Champion, Commonwealth Games Champion, etc. etc.). Indeed, combined with the shenanigans of the crowd and the stands, I was most definitely on the verge of a nervous breakdown! So, you can imagine how I felt when – on the second point of the match – Mike went into what appeared to be a complete and utter meltdown of vitriolic rage. It stemmed from a long rally ending with a beautifully accurate winning smash from Mike, which dissected the tramlines almost perfectly and which was at least six inches inside the line. The call from the home country linesman was "OUT" with fiercely outstretched arms signalling this decision. It was an outrageous call, and clearly to Mike it was a signal of future intent. He exploded into a tantrum of rage and went around every single one of the court officials / line judges individually, one by one, letting them know in no uncertain terms, in an extremely loud and aggressive voice, his opinions of their performance so far and what he expected moving forwards.

I stood in the centre of the court – very alone – bewildered and literally gobsmacked as to what was unfolding in front of me. I was left wondering what I had done to deserve this, and how my partner could possibly recover from this level of emotional outrage to continue the match. Well, after what seemed an eternity, Mike returned back to join me in the centre of the court where he could see I was a mess! Calmly as you like, he winked at me and said, "Don't worry, relax, all the calls will go our way from now onwards."

Sure enough, we got the benefit of any close decisions from that point onwards. Unbeknownst to me, Mike knew exactly what he was doing and was in complete control of his emotions throughout the whole episode. With such talent, Mike was definitely Hollywood's loss!

# Reviewing matches

You can have lots of experiences, but unless you reflect on them, you're not going to learn much. This is why we recommend reviewing your matches. To reflect on your capability in responding to match events effectively, you first need to decide what the critical events were and then review your responses.

These events needn't be events that became turning points, although they are important. They can be events, for example, where the response to a potential negative turning point was so good that the potentially critical event had no effect on the journey of the match. Once the events have been agreed, you can judge how effective your response was.

There are various tools to help you do this; for example, reviewing a video from the match. Of course, for many players, the option of reviewing a video is not available. Therefore, the sheet below can be used as a reflection tool, post-match, to identify how you responded to certain events and how you would have liked to have responded.

A very good way to use this sheet is for you and your coach to fill it out separately, and compare how you saw the match and your responses afterwards. It can be the basis for a very good discussion.

| Match: | Date: | Venue: |
|---|---|---|
| Opposition: | Conditions: | |

| Score | Match Event | Response | Knock-on effects |
|---|---|---|---|
| | | | |

This sheet can be used from match to match, recording a variety of events and responses. Match events that could become potential turning points can be any incident; by focussing on the effectiveness of your response, you can *control the controllable* (rather than the event itself, which is not always controllable).

It's a good idea to aim for a standard response through a standard routine, which you will use throughout the match, known in racket sports as an 'in-between point routine'.

As psychological skills help clear the mind for the decision-making involved with action, it's normal for a routine to include elements such as a relaxation technique, a quick review of what just happened, and a refocusing and activation technique – all in a defined sequence which can be repeated after each match event. There is an example in the first case study, below, but they are individual, and you can work with your coach or sport psychologist to work out your own.

This routine, when trained, will become second nature but may also need to be adapted for certain situations. That's because – once you have used this sheet in several matches over a sustained period – you may well begin to see patterns emerge and identify clear priorities. These priorities may require more specific plans. Here's an example.

## Case Study

A player, let's call her Alice, had lost five matches in the last three months when she had won the first game and built up a lead in the second game playing in a relaxed manner. In the early passages of play, Alice stuck to her game plan and game identity only to become increasingly tense and erratic in her decision-making as her opponents came back. In each match, she eventually lost the second game in hard-fought contests, each time having been within a couple of points of victory (and on three occasions having had match point). The final game was always much less competitive, with the opposition winning easily.

The identified 'game event' in each case was failing to close out the match successfully, following which the opposition grew in confidence and saw the possibility of winning; even though the match score was all-square in the second game, it felt like the momentum had swung irreversibly.

Opposite is an example of one of the match event sheets:

| Score | Match Event | Response | Knock-on effects |
|-------|-------------|----------|------------------|
| 21-17 20-16 | Match point lost by being too passive | Negative self-talk and negative body language. A look of 'here we go again' | Decision making became more desperate; rushed in-between points and the opponent grew in confidence |

As a result of the match analysis sheet above, Alice can formulate an action plan for the next match. Here's an example; it includes an extra column headed "Match Flow insights".

| Area | Heading | Action | Match Flow Insights |
|------|---------|--------|---------------------|
| Tactical | Impose your game | To stay with the game plan that got you into the winning position. As the Americans say, "Dance with the one that brought ya!" | Any worthwhile opponent will attempt to put pressure on at the end. They will not throw in the towel, and you are unlikely to win by hoping they miss. |
| Mental | Routine | Use standard routine: (Release, Review, Reset; or similar) | Expect and relish tough moments. |

| Measure | Through match charting and/or video: |
|---|---|
| | - Analysis of the implementation of the game plan and patterns of play when serving for the match |
| | - Analysis of in-between point routine |

# Case Study

In a separate case study, Charles is a very talented player and – when in the right frame of mind – can play to a very high, almost unplayable level, often going through sustained periods of being 'in the zone'. He can get easily distracted, though, and opponents have started to play on this to try to distract him. In recent matches, Charles has become distracted by the crowd, who is watching, and (in particular) is very sensitive to biased clapping in favour of the opposition.

This has cost a number of matches recently, which is frustrating for both the player and his supporters, as there is an element of self-destruction about things. In turn, there is a feeling that the skill level required to beat Charles is much greater than the easy ploy of simple distraction, and Charles submits too easily to distraction.

Opposite is an example of one of Charles's match event sheets:

| Score | Match Event | Response | Knock-on effects |
|---|---|---|---|
| 20-19 | Missed a comfortable smash at game point up, and the opposition's family and coach clapped loudly and for an extended period | Visibly distracted from the game and lost focus, losing the next two points quickly to lose the game in setting. | Took too long to become competitive again. Still looking at opposition's camp at 1-6 down in the second game. |

| Area | Heading | Action | Match Flow Insights |
|---|---|---|---|
| Mental | Attentional control | Bring attention to the here and now by bringing eyes to racket strings and listening to breathing. Refocus on the plan for the first shot of the next rally. | If your opponent can't win on the battlefield, they might try to entice you onto a different battlefield – a gamesmanship battlefield – particularly on a big point. Do not be tempted to go there. Stay on your battlefield. |
| Mental | Routine | Use existing routine | |
| Measure | Through match charting and/or video:<br>- Visible use of routine<br>- Competitiveness during rallies as defined by shot selection and winning points that demand extra effort. | | |

It might also be that a player needs a specific plan depending on the type of opponent they are facing. Often, players are more comfortable when facing an opponent they perceive to be better than they are... there is a feeling that they are 'hunting' for the victory with everything to be gained.

On the flip side, it is not unusual for players to be less comfortable against players who they feel they are expected to beat; therefore, there is as much to lose as to be gained. A lot of this is down to perspective and, therefore, reframing may be a skill worth employing. There is more on how to reframe things in the section, 'Have your own ranking system'.

## Key points to remember

- There are times in a match when you can zoom out to see the bigger picture by assessing the state of play.

- The state of play is a snapshot of where you think the balance of the match is at a given point; it allows you to consider different routes to victory.

- It takes into account the stage of momentum, the score, and the tactical picture.

- Responding to match events is critical to controlling momentum.

- Identifying important match events allows you to assess your response in post-match reviews.

# Chapter 6: Your Tactical Game

As we have seen, momentum shifts quickly when both sides' performances move simultaneously – one being boosted, and the other being diminished. As we have also seen, this can happen dramatically after significant match events that can become turning points, with the gap widening quickly, or it can happen more steadily over a period of time as one side gains dominance with superior performance. This superior performance is often achieved through the execution of effective tactics.

The tactical match-up – *on paper* – may appear to favour one side, but how each side executes their tactics and their timing is significant. With an effective strategy, the difference in the sides – according to rankings or league position – can be changed considerably if the weaker side successfully uses their strengths against the weaknesses of the better side, or if they limit the strengths of the better side – reducing their ability, as shown by the red line on the graphic below.

## Your game in focus

As we've already established, the changes to be made will fall into either the tactical or mental area, and we'll look at these in greater detail in a moment. However, the changes will centre around your level of performance, including how you are feeling and whether you are getting your game into gear compared to usual. These will be alongside how your strengths and weaknesses match up with the strengths and weaknesses of the opposition.

Before examining some of the tactical and mental adaptations you can make in different phases, and how you can adapt your performance, let's take a closer look at some of the tactical and mental skills you need to know before going into a match.

We'll start by looking at your game, and then widen the discussion into considerations and options during the match.

**How well do you know your game?**

Having a *clear game identity* is critical to performing well in matches for the following reasons:

- To get your game up and running, on the court, at the start of the match
- To judge the effectiveness of your performance
- To create a game plan for different opponents
- To vary or adapt things when you choose
- To impose your game on the opposition

There are many comprehensive tactical and mental frameworks in sport that cover all aspects of both mental and tactical areas.

These are often produced by governing bodies or from academic research where the overriding aim is to produce something which allows for all possibilities. There are, equally, a range of approaches that are currently 'in fashion' or which come from a specific angle.

The value *for you*, however, is not to know everything that could happen and every tactic that could be exploited; it is to know what *you* find most appropriate to you and your game in the situations you find yourself in most often.

*An example of a player who has a clear idea of his game plan is Viktor Axelsen from Denmark.*

Once you know your own game well, then you have a good base from which to make decisions.

Now, let's look at the right tactics and mental approach for *your* game.

# Your tactical approach

There is no tactical approach that suits all match situations, arenas, and styles of opponent. Making the right tactical decisions at the right time can make the difference between a 16-16 battle and a 21-16 win. But what are the right tactics, and when is the right time?

## The right tactics

At the core of deciding the right tactics for you is deciding what your strengths and weaknesses are. Before you can impose your own game, or step it up a level, or vary from it, you have to know what your own game is.

To help you decide, imagine how your perfect rally would look, a rally that you could repeat. Work through the following game situations thinking about your court positioning. What would you do on the first shot in each of the situations below? The second shot? If you were in a rally, how would you want it to end?

- When serving to the T.

- When serving out wide.

- When returning against an opponent's best serve.

- When returning a flick serve.

- When in a rally when you are under fierce attack.

- When you are controlling the net.

- When your opponents are charging the net.

By doing this, you will come up with your favourite repeatable patterns for your badminton.

Here are two common examples:

1. If someone is catching you out with a very deceptive flick serve, you may choose to stand just a few inches further back on your return of serve court position to enable you to cover the flick and therefore the movement backwards more effectively.

2. If your opponents are charging the net very effectively and putting pressure on your defence, you must be aware at all times to go over them and exploit the gaps

they leave behind them when charging forwards. So, utilise a higher, more passive defence style to push them backwards and be ready to use the net again soon with flatter, firmer defensive blocks and fades when the opportunity presents itself.

Why are repeatable patterns important? Well, as stated earlier, if you know what they are, then you have a base from which to work, from which to make tactical decisions. It is also true that the nearest thing to a pure comparison of levels happens when one player's repeatable patterns are pitched against the other player's repeatable patterns. When both players get their game on the court at the same time, you can tell who is more likely to win (if that player is able to achieve this consistently). The player who controls the repeatable patterns is usually the player who will end up with the momentum sooner or later.

*Variations* are when you do something that departs from these repeatable patterns. They can be done intentionally by switching the play, or unintentionally with a one-off lucky shot. A variation is different to the way you usually play and has probably caught your opponent unawares. Variations are usually less reliable than repeatable patterns and may not come off. But when they do, they can interrupt the flow of a match and may alter it significantly.

To help establish your tactical approach, why not work through the following questions to decide what your 'blueprint' approach would be.

# Blueprint matches (tactical)

Think about three recent matches that you would like to represent your style of play. They should be matches that took place within the last year or so, that you can clearly recall.

They should be competitive matches where you played well, and represent the type of play you feel could be regularly achieved. Of course, they should contain identifiable patterns of play which are repeatable.

Thinking about these matches in more depth now, consider the following questions.

- What tactical strengths would have been obvious to a neutral coach watching from the stands?

- How did these tactical strengths result in superior performance against the opposition?

- If the neutral coach was to describe your performance to the press, what would they say? Make a list of words and phrases they might use.

Now think about how you can turn this information into an action plan:

- What steps do you need to take to implement this tactical approach in upcoming matches?

- How can you not just implement but *impose* it on the opposition in matches?

- What might prevent you from implementing this approach in upcoming matches? What are the challenges?

- How can you best prepare to impose your tactical approach on the opposition in your next match?

# Adjusting your game

Once you have identified your approach, it would be fantastic just to implement it exactly as you envisage... maintaining high levels of mental and tactical application throughout the match by playing in a bubble without the requirement to make any adjustments. This isn't easy to achieve because – as we know – very few matches happen like that.

As with any journey, you have to make adjustments as you go along based on the state of the game – sometimes small, sometimes a little bigger. You will need to make adjustments to your game in response to:

- The score

- Your expectations of your playing level

- The developing tactical battle

- Match events

- The phase of momentum

Although these are listed separately, in reality they can be interconnected. For example, you may be aware that you are performing below your level and not playing the way you envisaged. As such, you want to become more aggressive, but you recognise the score is in your favour and that the opposition are nervous and ineffective with time running out for them. Therefore, the state of the game tells you that it would be the wrong time to try to step up a gear as you'll probably win with your current level. Matches are full of these kinds of decisions, and (as we'll see later) assessing the state of the game is a good starting point.

First, though, let's take a quick tour of some of the tactical and mental tools you can use to make adjustments. The following sections are some of the tools and processes we've found useful, though not all will apply to your game.

## Decide your strategy and game plan

You are setting out to win, but how? What is your strategy? For example, do you plan to take the game to the opposition and win the game by forcing errors or, alternatively to sit back, play defensively and wait for their unforced errors

Strategy may be seen as planning the overall management of a game to achieve the required result; it directs the game plan. The game plan is more defined and is the chosen way of implementing the strategy, in other words the tactics that you aim to execute on court.

The two strategies in the example above will lead to different game plans – containing different tactics – depending on the individual strengths and weaknesses of the players.

## Get your game in play

This begins with knowing your game (see previous pages) and having a clear idea of the level you'd like to perform at. Then it is all about the successful execution of this game plan. If you are successful at imposing your game on the opposition early then this can build momentum for you right from the start.

Not getting your game into gear early in the match can be for a variety of reasons, including not warming up effectively, nerves, the opposition's tactics preventing you, feeling out of sorts, etc., etc. If you know yourself well and observe what happens regularly to you at the start of matches, then you can develop strategies to improve. In Chapter 8, there is a great example of how the GB Olympic team recognised this and the strategies they implemented to get off to a fast start.

## Imposing your game

Central to the tactical battle in most matches is who imposes their game on the opposition. It comes down to simple maths – percentages to be precise – one side getting to do more of what they want to do, more often. For example, if a player or team has success attacking a certain side, then they need to do that more often during the match and especially at critical moments (often related to the score).

## Tactical thinking

Through fighting spirit and renewing your efforts, you will become a tough competitor in the heat of the battle. However, you have to make sure you are fighting the right battle. All the mental skills required to fight hard may not have been required had you simply realised you were playing to your opponent's strengths. This might be playing too much of a lifting game as opposed to using the net more.

## Stick or Twist

There may come a point in a match when you have to decide whether you will stick to your plan or change it. Maybe you have established a lead with your plan, but now the momentum is beginning to turn, possibly due to a significant match event or perhaps due to a change in the opposition's tactics. You may even have fallen behind in the score. How do you decide whether to change, or do what you were doing better? Here's a great way to decide, based on knowing how well you are executing your plan.

> "If you're behind, but you're actually playing really well, and you're executing a game plan but you're still losing, then you might need to change.
>
> If you are performing averagely, and if you can just execute on a higher level now, then you can switch the momentum in your favour."
>
> Nathan Robertson

## Tempo

Tempo can play an important role in gaining or killing and then regaining momentum. When you hear on the news that momentum is building for, say, a peace process or the call for climate change, it usually refers to the fact that a series of events – seen as positive to the cause – have happened in a short space of time. Equally, when you hear that the same thing is losing momentum, it means that few positive events – or possibly a series of negative events – have happened in quick succession.

What is important here is the series of events *in quick succession*. Let's revisit and combine this with what we know about the feel of momentum when it's with you or against you. When momentum is for you, you feel good, win the close points, decisions seem easy, etc. The reverse is true when momentum is against you. So, it follows that you want events to happen quickly (as they are likely to be positive) when momentum is for you, and fewer events to happen when momentum is against you. Therefore, the tempo at which you play becomes an important way to influence momentum.

## Actor or reactor

When a player is the actor, they are instigating the play and making the shots, as opposed to reacting to the moves the opposition is making. Players who wait for the opposition to make the play are described as being reactive or passive.

As the match progresses, it's worth keeping an eye on who is the actor and who is the reactor within the points. Being the actor keeps the future in your hands but may mean taking more risks than a passive player. Either tactic is valid, and you may need both at different times. For example, there is an argument for being more passive when you see the opposition is nervous, and there is an argument for being the actor when you want to drive home your advantage against a better player.

## Carrying a threat

Whatever your game style, carrying a threat is important when it comes to controlling momentum. Even when a player is down in the match, if they carry a tactical threat such as a big weapon, or a mental threat such as the ability to suddenly get fired up, it can be unsettling for the opposition who are trying to maintain momentum. Carrying a threat means a turning point is more likely to happen in your favour, so look to your own game and *decide what threats you carry*.

## Brilliance – Outrageous Skill – Momentum Deflator!

### by Andy Wood

Whilst sitting in the coach's chair, courtside, trying to support our players through a critical match, I have to admit (on rare occasions) to being completely deflated by an opponent's sheer brilliance. If *I* felt that… goodness only knows what my player felt!

Imagine having played almost the perfect rally and having just delivered what you thought was your final winning shot only to see your opponent deliver a piece of sublime skill, creating a shot that you didn't believe was possible, or which you had never even seen before. You have to suffer the indignity and humiliation of watching the shuttle drift past you and landing on a part of the court that was impossible to cover.

There is no doubt that these moments create potential turning points. If you were coming up against the likes of Kevin Sukamuljo, Trikus Herryanto, Sigit Budiarto, or Eng Hian, then you'd better have a level of acceptance that these moments can and will occur, and have a strategy to combat how you might feel when they do.

The Indonesian players, in particular, are known for their outrageous skill and ability with the racket. Rexy Mainaky, the former Olympic and World Champion who spent several years in the UK as part of our GB Coaching team, did an excellent job in helping our players acquire some of these skills. He explained that the Indonesian training centres are often residential with the players all sleeping in large dormitories. In the evenings, already after a hard day's training, the youngsters get a little restless and bored – with not much to do in their downtime. So, they simply get back onto the courts and have a few hours of 'free' play with no coaches, no instruction, no drilling, or anything systematic. They experiment with creating trick shots, making up new skill games, and having fun trying to outmanoeuvre each other with flair. Pure unadulterated freedom, fun, and creativity exploring the sport!

*Kevin Sukamuljo (Indonesia).*

## Consistency

The effect of consistency on the flow of the match can be enormous. If you do not miss, the impact on your opponent can be significant. If they know that, in order to beat you, they are going to have to keep their badminton above your level of consistency for a long period of time, then their confidence can drop; even a consistent player may start to make errors.

The effect is like that of an arm wrestle. If you keep the pressure on for long enough, then the opponent will wilt. Some sooner, some later, depending on how mentally tough they are.

This is shown if you chart a match's points won and lost in a row. You will often see close, hard-fought periods followed by one player losing a string of quicker points, before the consistent battle continues. How you manipulate these runs of points is often decisive in who wins the game, and one way you can do this is by controlling the margins.

## Control your margins – play your margins card!

Consciously decide upon the level of your margins consistently throughout the match.

You may be an offensive, aggressive player that loves an attacking game with high risk and you are used to hitting within half an inch of the line and brushing the net tape. Or you may be a more passive, patient player that prefers long, hard rallies and much safer shot selections. Either way, the match conditions will determine a need to adjust your risk-taking in terms of accuracy and reliability. You want to prevent gifting any free points to your opponent by making avoidable errors.

It is usual at the start of a match, for instance, to have slightly higher margins until you get completely comfortable with the arena and conditions and opponent's style of play. As the match progresses, and hopefully as soon as possible, you can tighten your margins; you can hit closer to the lines and tighter to the tape to increase pressure on your opponent.

The risk versus reward ratio is a constant consideration in this situation, as you will have to make frequent decisions on how hard to push it. If you are feeling 'in the zone' – moving well, seeing the shuttle well, feeling invincible and full of confidence – you are likely to be playing with very fine margins. But if you are carrying a slight injury, in a new arena with poor vision and a drift, then you are likely to play safer, with caution, and utilise higher margins around your shot selection to ensure that you get a foothold within the match by not gifting free points to your opponent.

As we have seen throughout the book already, the match conditions, the momentum and flow, and the levels of confidence of both competitors are a constantly moving picture. Therefore, the need to constantly assess the level of risk in your decision making becomes paramount, as does the need to 'control your margins'.

## Tracking the patterns

As you progress through the match, you should learn to absorb information about the opposition, observing their favourite patterns, and mentally noting the pattern of their serving, returning, etc. This gives you match intelligence for later on, when the score could be crucial and a correct decision could tip the match in your favour. Very often, top players are aware of what has gone before, and are in a stronger position when it comes to the crunch because of it.

## Adapt your game to their game

Once you know your repeatable patterns, it is clearly advantageous to pit them against your opponent's game. All players have strengths and weaknesses, and many tactics can be used to exploit their weaknesses or avoid their strengths.

Individual weaknesses/strengths can be related to a variety of issues and we will not focus on them all here. Clearly, technique can be a limiting factor for some players and – usually – it is possible to work out their favourite and least favourite shots. Whatever their strengths or weaknesses – as long as it doesn't detract from your repeatable patterns – you should normally aim to give them what they don't like. For example, you flick players who have limited smash power.

*Limit their favourite patterns.* This works because as well as effectively playing a weaker opponent (one without use of their favourite patterns), when their favourite pattern is not winning them points, they can lose hope. Similarly, when they get cheap points from them, their confidence soars. For example, keep net players away from the net; don't make silly errors against consistent players; make every return against consistently accurate servers.

If you have mastered the knowledge of the opponent's repeatable patterns, you can gain an edge by calculated risk-taking on their sequences.

When concentrating on the opponent's game, do not forget about your own game. To keep things simple in the heat of the battle, you are often better off letting the opposition worry about how to deal with your imposing game. Being the initiator of the play is crucial if you want to keep the future in your own hands; usually, it's the first three shots of the rally that decide who takes charge of the point.

Nathan Robertson is the most exceptional example of a player who could play three or four shots ahead within the rally. By this, I mean he could carry out stroke production whilst calculating and creating a 'kill' opportunity in his mind that he could engineer some four shots later. Each of his shot selections would ultimately lead to that defining moment.

# Key points to remember

- Know your own game. What are your repeatable patterns?

- Be aware of your opponent's strengths and weaknesses – play smarter.

- Use simple thought processes to consider tactics, e.g., am I the actor or reactor? Am I imposing my game?

- Know when and how to adjust your game, especially in response to changing circumstances.

# Chapter 7: Your Mental Game

Momentum moves quickly when one player's level of performance drops, and their opponent's picks up. Arguably the biggest influence on your performance is your *state of mind*; it can affect all other performance factors. Your mental state can tighten up your technique, it can lead to poor decision making, and it can even overcome physical tiredness!

The trick of controlling momentum is the speed at which you renew your efforts and maintain the consistency of your ideal mental state. Now, you might be thinking that 'renewing efforts' suggests things will go wrong in the match, and this approach is a little pessimistic! Well, we can agree that if you stay in the zone for the whole match – so that nothing goes wrong – that's ideal. However, it remains true that matches rarely progress smoothly. Matches rarely take a straight line of improvement throughout – where everything gets better and better before the match finishes on a high. They don't progress good... very good... great... game over!

Let's look at your own experience in more detail, to check if this is true for you. How many matches have you played in your life? Work it out as matches per month on average and then multiply by 12 to find the number of matches per year, and then multiply that number by the number of years you've competed for. Bearing in mind that some years will have seen more matches than others, you will arrive at an approximate number.

Now, take a moment to consider how many of that number, in fact, went "good ... very good... great... game over". And we should state that we mean competitive matches, not one-sided ones. We imagine there will be a few memorable ones, but people usually don't have very many. Now work out this number as a percentage of total matches. If you follow the usual pattern of responses we experience with players and former players, then the percentage is rarely more than 10% and often just 1 or 2%.

Therefore, if we turn things around, we can say that 90+% of your matches will have contained different phases, some of which are likely to be testing. They will encompass events that may be very challenging, such as missed opportunities, missed easy shots, or bad line calls against you. This is where the mental side of the game is critical.

A 95% - 5% quote was offered by Brad Gilbert, former coach to Andy Murray and Andre Agassi, in his book "Winning Ugly" where he states: "In competition amongst equally matched Elite level performers, 5% of the time your opponent is in the zone and you won't win; 5% of the time, you are in the zone and can't lose. But the other 90% of the time, it's up for grabs; there is a way to win. You've just got to figure out what it is…"

# Renewing your efforts

Renewing efforts is an individual thing. It does not necessarily mean a lot of visible bustle and bluster. In fact, immediately renewing efforts can be an internal, unemotional, professional decision. It is important to know your own mental and emotional bandwidth, and your strategies to keep things at an optimal level throughout the full duration of the contest.

Finding the right state for you – on court – is what is important. People are different and play well in different states. Some like to be energised the whole time; others prefer to be calmer and more reflective until it matters. You must decide how *you* want to be on court. Later, in this chapter, there is advice for getting your mental state right before you go onto court (see 'Have your own ranking system').

# Gail Emms

By Andy Wood

It soon became abundantly clear to our coaching team that in order for Gail Emms to perform at her 'destructive' best in competitive matches, she needed a big 'IN' to a match. By this, I mean she needed to make something happen in the very early stages of the match, to create a significant event or piece of play which signalled to her (and her opponents) that 'SHE' would be in charge of proceedings today.

This could be a dynamic interception or an explosive kill off the tape at the net, or a winning crouch defence drive from her opposing man's very best smash.

Creating this event or 'IN' in the early stages became a pivotal factor as two very different Gail Emms could emerge into the match. One of which was full of confidence, aggressive, destructive and capable of almost single-handedly obliterating her opponents. Or the other, who was passive, safe, reserved and unsure.

There was no doubting which Gail Emms we all preferred and which one her partners needed to show up. Much time was spent within her partnerships trying to manipulate and create this event or 'IN' to the match successfully. On the majority of occasions, Gail managed to achieve this, and it unquestionably, in turn, had a significant effect on her ability to acquire and control the momentum of the match.

It is important to know that Gail Emms was a very proactive, aggressive, attacking player who was always looking to play that 'killer' shot and hit winners. Her natural style was to take calculated risks, gamble on interceptions, and dominate her opponents by being offensive and not allowing them to settle. When confronted with this approach very early on in a match, it can be very difficult for an opponent to find a foothold; before you know it, you are being swept away.

Almost always, at the highest level, when I charted Gail's matches, her unforced error rate would be slightly higher than the other three players on the court. However, when it came to her numbers on 'winning shots', she would inevitably be significantly higher than the others, and it was this element of her game that was most disruptive to her opponents and so difficult to face. It became imperative that Gail adopted and maintained this aggressive, high-risk approach in order to maximise her performance. The fact that she would make a higher number of justifiable errors (and would need to accept that) became a regular discussion topic.

# Blueprint matches (mental)

Think about three recent matches which you would like to represent your ideal mental state. They should be matches that took place within the last year or so, in order to clearly recall them.

Thinking about these matches in more depth now, and consider the following questions:

- What mental qualities would have been obvious to a neutral coach watching from the stands?

- How did this approach result in superior performance to the opposition?

- If the neutral coach was to describe your mental performance to the press, what would they say? Make a list of words and phrases they might use.

Now think about how you turn the information above into an action plan:

- How can you best prepare to implement this mental approach in upcoming matches?

- Did you follow a specific strategy to achieve this in these matches?

# Mental Tools

Below is a quick overview of the tools, compiled with the help of Sport Psychologist Ana Soares, that have proved successful in top sport. This list cannot do much more than identify tools that you might think will work for you. If you're interested, we suggest you explore them individually with your coach or with a sport psychologist.

## Self-talk

Self-talk is the stream of thoughts that we have running in our heads. These thoughts can be telling us positive things that can help our performance, or they can be telling us things that hinder our performance. They can be related to the match we are playing, or we might be thinking about what's for dinner.

Learning to control this stream of thoughts, and replacing negative thoughts with positive thoughts or phrases, is known as *positive self-talk*.

## Routines

Routines are a sequence of behaviours that allow you to be fully prepared and in-the-moment, ready to play. A routine is not only about the behaviours you do, but also about the thoughts that go alongside the behaviours.

A routine will also consist of a set of behaviours and thoughts and – ideally – be planned to allow more time to critically think about strategies and adapt to specific situations, including the phase of momentum.

## Visualisation

Visualisation is about seeing something in your head. It is not about daydreaming, though. It is a tool that you use *with a purpose*. It can be used to practise a specific skill in your head, such as a forehand or, for example, to help you prepare your strategy for the next point or a match.

## Goal setting

Before a match, you might have set some goals. You may want to exercise a wide variety of service strokes, for example. Or, you might want to make sure you take the shuttle really early at the net. Goal setting is about these types of goals, and can help you tactically or when you need to deal with specific turning points in a match.

## Activation/relaxation

Sometimes, you will need to calm yourself down. At other times, you might feel too lethargic and you need to get yourself more active during the match. Breathing exercises, for example, can help you achieve both of these states.

## Reframing

Reframing is about seeing a situation in a different way. Imagine you are one set up, and 3-4 down in the second set. You might feel that this is an unfavourable score, but if it was the beginning of the match, would you take this score? It can also be helpful to view a situation through the eyes of a third party. For example, how would a good friend see this situation?

# The mental battle

As important as the tactical, on-court battle is, the *mental* battle is equally relevant; it revolves around how both players respond to match events. Of course, no one does so inside their own bubble – players are watching each other and picking up signals about how the opposition is feeling, which can affect performance and, therefore, momentum.

Let's take a look at the role body language and 'energy' on the court can play in this battle.

## Body language

How you feel inside is reflected in your body language. Good body language – in-between points – is generally considered to involve a positive walk, a strong look, chin up, shoulders back with the racket head up. Poor body language is generally considered to be the opposite (e.g., drooping shoulders and head, slow walk, negative self-talk).

Body language plays a big part in controlling the energy on court. It affects both your energy and your opponent's energy.

Your own energy is affected by your body language because you tend to feel the way you act. With clothes, when you look good, you feel good, and vice versa. With friends, if you hang around with low, negative energy people, you may be affected, and vice versa. It's the same with body language; if you act as if you have low, negative energy, then you will probably make matters worse. High energy is what you want… preferably positive energy!

Body language also affects your opponent. Seeing poor body language can be a great boost to a player. Your opponent may not believe in their strength, but they will be encouraged by any signs of *your* weakness. Alternatively, seeing strong body language may cause your opponent to have doubts as to whether they can beat you, with no help from you.

Body language often reflects what players are feeling inside, but this is not always the case. The body language of players on court can vary depending on whether or not they know their opponent. For example, in junior national badminton, where players nearly always know their opponent, the accepted ranking order can affect things. The underlying power of these ranking orders, at national level, blurs the importance of body language. For example, a better player, when threatened with aggressive body language from a player lower in the ranking order, may respond with a disinterested look. A hint to their opponent to remember their place!

However, if you are playing abroad, you may not know your opponent – they could be a club player playing well, or the country's brightest young hope. Body language, therefore, becomes very important at international level (or when you don't know the opposition) because the only information an opponent may have about you is the information you provide. If you look good technically, tactically, and physically, their only hope is that you have mental weaknesses.

If you look calm and in control, while your opponent plays their best badminton, it gives them the message that they have to keep up that level all the way to the winning post. It suggests that you will be ready to pounce as soon as they drop their level and this, in itself, can raise doubts in their mind.

It is also extremely important for juniors to invest time and effort in practising positive body language at all times so that it becomes a habit. At senior level, tactics, technique, and fitness tend to have equalled themselves out, and matches are won and lost more on who is the better player mentally and tactically *on the day*.

Sharp international competitors watch their opponents and pick up signals of their mental energy in body language. If they pick up signals that *you* think the wheels are about to come off *your* performance, the only conclusion they can draw is that you are afraid it will happen – that you have a habit of falling apart. This will be the case, particularly if the negative vibes have a 'here we go again' feel. This only encourages your opponent.

There are two simple lessons to be learned from this:

1. If you want to succeed at a higher level, learn to control your body language. You can use the mental tools listed above to help control your energy between points.

2. Watch the body language of your opponent, and remember to keep doing it. This is easy in boxing because you are only a few feet away; in badminton, you have to look closely and regularly if you want to pick up any signals. Many turning points will occur in the mind of your opponent. You may not know what causes them, but you can sense them if you keep an eye on how your opponent is feeling. The key is to watch them regularly and not just after really obvious potential turning points.

A word of warning: opponents can sometimes put on an act. Look out for this and be particularly sceptical if their body language is a bit too contrived… lulling players into a false sense of security is an old trick!

Rafael Nadal is an excellent example of a competitor who imposes his energy and aura of invincibility on his opponent. He routinely makes his opponent wait before the toss of the coin whilst he lines up his armoury and his drinks bottles! He then explodes onto the court, galloping ruthlessly like El Toro – 'The Bull' – straight towards you.

*Rafael Nadal.*

You must be prepared to set the energy level on the court, not just react to it. This might mean being the first in the match to show really positive energy in your body language when all is quiet around you. It may mean taking your time when your opponent wants to hurry. It may mean not dropping energy when your opponent does. This can happen when you have battled hard to establish a lead and your opponent's energy drops. The lead seems big enough, so you can find yourself copying the energy level coming from the other side of the net. The problem is that your opponent may increase their energy first, and you can be slow to react, still thinking, "It'll be all right; I have a big lead." This is what coaches mean when they say, "Don't relax if you get in front".

This change in energy can have a big effect on a match if it is timed to coincide with a turning point. We have even seen older players lull younger players into a false sense of security this way – they lose a few consecutive points in a set and appear to give up towards the end of the set only to come out for the start of the next set (an ideal turning point in itself) totally fired up.

It is a cunning plan to make the energy levels on court drop when you are losing. It's called *letting the match go flat*. It suits the person who is behind, because if they were losing when the energy was high, they can't do any worse when it goes flat. They then wait until a key time approaches and raise their energy levels quickly to catch the opponent napping. It is a bit like being behind in a running race and shouting "stop" and slowing down, then as the opponent begins to slow down, shouting "go" and overtaking them.

# Momentum and current form

The mental state of a player is often affected by the current form of their opponent.

A lesser player who is having a good run of form is obviously going to renew their efforts quicker and keep renewing them because their confidence is generally high. This is because confidence is linked closely to belief in being able to do a task. Players on form, with some good recent results, have greater belief than normal. This keeps their mental energy higher for longer, as recent experiences tell them it's worth it.

Similarly, players who are having a poor run of form often find momentum swings against them more quickly. This is because they lose heart quicker, which prevents them from renewing their efforts as quickly or for as long; recent experiences tell them it's not worth it.

Here is an example of this:

In a recent international match, a player lost 20-22, 21-12, 21-12. This player was rusty due to injury and nervous about her lack of any recent form. She was all right as long as things went for her. When they went against her, she lost belief quickly, as the score suggests.

# Momentum and personalities

Another factor that can affect how momentum moves in a match is the personality of your opponent.

Most players are strongest in one stage of momentum and more vulnerable in others. For example, some players look invincible when they have the flow with them, but sometimes you may only have to get a small lead for their attitude – and consequently their play – to deteriorate.

Some reactive players are terrific when they are behind, showing tenacious fighting qualities, but then seem to lose these qualities when they get in front. They don't seem to be comfortable being the one who is out in the lead. They prefer to battle from behind.

*Chen Long (L) of China is a great example of a player who has secured many victories after coming from behind in matches. Kento Momota (R) is another.*

Some characters in badminton are fatalistic and tend to see turning points as marking the beginning of a disaster. Their heads can go down very quickly once the flow goes against them, with a feeling of 'this always happens to me'. Such players typically do not understand momentum; they often have a superstitious view of it and think it normally only turns dramatically. For this reason, they are as capable of dramatic comebacks as dramatic losses in momentum.

Some players seem to play terribly until the momentum is neutral, and they just seem to find the right shot at the right time. These types of players often *nearly* lose to players they shouldn't lose to, but always just seem to pull through.

Other players are more emotional, and able to change their energy in a flash, and sudden changes in energy are common with Danish badminton players. The Danish club system is exceptional for developing talent and an awareness of competitive opportunities within match play. Each young, talented player progresses through the club's development, surrounded by ex-international and world-class players of all ages who 'stay' in the game because of their love of the sport. This constant interaction and learning from an experienced pool of knowledge creates tactically astute and competitively aware players who can change energy and focus extremely quickly.

They can create turning points simply because of their ability to change energy and focus quickly – they can be missing everything and feeling sorry for themselves one minute, and then be on fire the next minute. These players typically have the ability to forget what's gone on before, and quickly step up their energy to sometimes take best advantage of the scoring system. (See the next chapter for an in-depth look at the scoring system.) This is why these players often turn matches around and are more successful than logic suggests they should be.

*Jan Jorgensen of Denmark.*

## Use this knowledge to be prepared

If you know the character of the player you are playing – and can recognise in which stage they are more effective – you are more likely to anticipate the tough points of the match and get ready accordingly.

For example, if your opponent is poor at closing out leads when things are going their way, then be prepared to take a lot of good play from them early on. You may not get a proper chance to win until you fight back from behind, so keep competing hard throughout each game. If they start to wobble, make them play a lot of shuttles so they have to earn their points.

If your opponent is known for starting slowly and always battling hard when behind, then be ready. Be prepared to raise your game, and don't expect things to be easy just because you have the lead.

In other matches, you may be playing a moody player. It is important not to provoke this type of player when they are feeling down and inward-looking. Let them dwell on their own problems while you stack up the points. A badly timed and intimidating "Come on" against these players could turn their attention to the battle and from how badly they are playing. This could be dangerous.

For example, basketball legend Michael Jordan, in the documentary "Last Dance", talked a lot about opponents 'fuelling his fire and stoking his desire"!

Think about the players you play against, or know. When do they play best? What can you do to defeat them when they are in their favourite stage? Become an expert on your opponents and your environment.

# Mental preparation

What makes badminton unpredictable is that badminton players do not always perform to a certain level, like machines. Players play better some days and worse others. It often depends on their mental state going into the match.

It is not uncommon to see matches where players roll over for opponents they consider to be better. It is also not uncommon to see the same players fighting as if their lives depend on it, in order to beat lower-ranked opposition. In the first case, they give too much respect to the higher-ranked player, while in the second, they fight harder than ever against the lower-ranked player because there are some people you just don't lose to.

In both situations, there is an underlying current of feeling that affects how the players play. To a large degree, it is produced by ranking systems that are external to the player – such as national rankings, county rankings, seedings, world rankings, and so on. Having a ranking system that is more individual to you, and which helps you view each match in the best possible way for you, is beneficial.

# Have your own ranking system

If a ranking system is going to work, it has to be based on badminton expertise – on an understanding of how badminton works – rather than simply on previous results. By using that understanding, it is possible to produce a scheme in which players fall into one of four categories:

1.  Very much worse than you (one-star match)
2.  A little bit worse than you (two-star match)

3. A little bit better than you (three-star match)

4. Very much better than you (four-star match)

In theory, you could have an extra category for players who are the same but, in reality, someone is nearly always the favourite.

This ranking system has psychological implications, and it is a system that can help you understand, in advance, how momentum might be managed in the matches.

Matches involving categories 1 and 4 are relatively straightforward to handle mentally. This is because you know what will happen, and the human mind is happiest when the situation is predictable. Humans find unpredictable situations scary (e.g., dark alleys, spiders, snakes).

In other words, if you are playing a player who is very much better than you (a four-star match), then you have little to lose, and everyone knows you have little to lose. If, for example, you are playing the number one seed in a major tournament, then – in one sense – you can't lose. If you get a good score, everyone will say, "Well done – you'll beat them next time" or "You're coming along really well". And if you lose heavily, it is no more than everyone expected. If you win, by contrast, you get rewarded with rankings points, publicity, and possibly prize money.

If your opponent is very much worse than you (a one-star match), then it is often a case of you settling your nerves as soon as you can, remaining focused, and cruising to a victory with relaxed badminton.

It is the second and third categories that provide particular challenges. In the case of the two-star and three-star matches, you really do not know what will happen.

Two-star matches can be particularly testing. Not only are they unpredictable, but the player you are playing is likely to be hunting you. It is not easy to play matches when you know that you are being hunted.

Even if you come through these uncomfortable feelings and win, the result will be no more than was expected. Even before the match, you may have people asking you who you are playing in the following match! Yet we should not forget that to win a tournament as a seeded player – even a Super Series tournament such as the All-England Championships or a World Tour event – you have to win a large number of two-star matches. Number one seeds, in particular, have to win multiple two-star matches, and have learned how to do so.

Three-star matches are also tough. But this time, you are hunting the opposition, and it is more comfortable mentally to be the hunter rather than the hunted. You still cannot easily predict what will happen, but it is challenging and you know that your opponent will probably be feeling more uncomfortable about the match than you. But, as with a two-star match, you are still in unknown territory and you have to deal with the unknown.

With all matches, you have approximately 40 minutes (the average length of a match currently) to work out what is going on, solve problems, and successfully come through the match. But you walk onto the court not knowing what is going to happen. The most successful players are those who learn to enjoy the *challenge* of the unknown.

It is also very important to make your own assessment of two and three-star wins. For example, if you have not played for three weeks because of injury and are entering a tournament with a heavy cold, your first match (according to the external rating system) may be a one-star match. But for you, at that particular point, it is a two-star match. You will get no credit for winning it but, if you do, you will know it was a good win.

Another example of a three-star win is where you win a match you are expected to win (e.g., a two-star match) when your form is poor. By your standards, it is a three-star win, even if the rankings tell a different story.

By learning to get your mind right before you play, you can begin to manage momentum before the match. This mental fitness is helped through mental preparation. The two-star matches are the most difficult of all, because you seemingly have nothing to win. So, become a badminton expert! Know that all badminton players find it tough to play well in these matches. In your own mind, make the two-star matches the ones to get psyched up for, for this reason. After all, if you win all these matches, you will always have a good season.

When Jimmy Connors, arguably one of the toughest competitors in tennis ever, was interviewed before a match he was expected to win, and asked about the outcome, he would usually say something like: I don't predict matches. I really don't know if I'm going to win. But I do know one thing. If the other guy's going to win, he'll have one hell of a fight on his hands. He'll have to work really hard.

Anthony Clark and Donna Kellogg took their partnership to another level once they mastered this way of thinking. They had a desperately poor preparation period for a major event in Asia where they were hellbent on doing well and announcing themselves as real contenders for the major World medals in mixed doubles. Everything that could possibly go wrong in the few weeks before the event did.

They both picked up minor injuries and illnesses, which severely impacted their preparation and their on-court training hours. It was touch and go whether they were well enough to travel, let alone compete. The actual start date of the event was one week after the flight, so the decision was made to take the flight and hope that there was some improvement in their health in the days before they took to the court. Clearly, this decision was a gamble, but it was one that paid off astronomically as the process went on to cement their *resilience* and *togetherness* as a partnership, making them stronger, more competitive, and incredibly hard to beat.

As the tournament got closer and closer, their wellbeing improved only marginally, and they took to the courts knowing that they were well below the normal 100% health levels, were carrying minor injuries, and were critically underprepared for a major, target event. So, nothing could be clearer than the fact that they were not going to win their opening match by being well-prepared, nor offering beautiful, physical badminton from two high-quality players at the very tops of their games. That method of winning was simply not an option.

So, what else did they have in their lockers? Well, actually, quite a lot – they had their 'guts' and fighting spirit. They had patience – they were prepared to stay out there forever if that's what it took to get the job done. They both had outstanding defences, making it extremely difficult for any opponents to actually put the shuttle on the floor (even off relatively easy kill opportunities). They had excellent 'basics' or fundamentals of the game (e.g., very effective serves and returns and good consistency levels). They had complete respect for each other's capabilities and fighting qualities. And they had well-developed badminton brains and situational awareness. The recognition of these qualities, then the focussed reliance upon them, together with 'acceptance' of the situation and the 'lowered sense of expectation', gave Anthony and Donna another level of competitiveness. This competitiveness and mindset took them all the way to the title even though they were certainly below 100% in their levels of health and fitness.

The realisation of these additional attributes, and the influence they actually had on their opponents' performances (once Anthony and Donna began to focus on them a little more), took away the pressure of having to deliver 'perfect' badminton all the time. Indeed, their performances in that tournament became the catalyst for numerous further titles; titles they won whilst having less than perfect preparation!

One astounding rally that epitomises this fighting spirit, and one I am sure every badminton enthusiast remembers vividly, was in the semi-finals of the All England Championships in 2007 against Xie Zhongbo and Zhang Yawen. Anthony and Donna managed to win a crucial rally despite Anthony playing three consecutive shots – and eventually a winner – from his seated position on the floor of the court after his original dive to retrieve the shuttle. This took the stuffing out of their Chinese opponents, helping them to move forwards and take their rightful place in the All England Final.

*Anthony Clark and Donna Kellogg.*

As a younger player, I always dreamed of playing the perfect match where I couldn't do anything wrong. The reality, however, is very different!

Anthony Clark

# Key points to remember

- Know your ideal mental state.
- Know when and how to adjust it to changing circumstances.
- Use your knowledge of Match Flow to stay positive and see opportunities.
- Renew your efforts quickly after a setback.
- Keep your body language positive.
- Prepare yourself mentally before the match.

# Chapter 8: Know The Score

Before setting off on any journey, you normally know the direction of travel, which roads to take, and the turns to make. In badminton, when you set off, you can never be sure which way the journey will go, especially if you are playing someone of a similar standard!

So, it is important to know the general landscape you are travelling over and the possible routes through it. Understanding that the match will flow through phases – giving players good patches and bad patches – is a useful start and is valid for all sports. But, of course, this does not happen independently of the scoring system.

To understand the impact of the developing score on the players, imagine for a moment two players of a similar standard playing badminton points *without* keeping track of the score. Imagine they play for an hour, changing server every five minutes with the sole intention of improving their badminton and developing rallies. There can be no pattern of the match because there is no match. Nonetheless, the standard of play of each player would go through patches, and as a result, the success of rally completion would ebb and flow due to a variety of influencing factors: mental, tactical, and physical.

However, the one thing that is *not* affecting them is the awareness of a match developing in one direction or the other. The score going for them or against them is not directing their thoughts, feelings, or behaviours.

If they were to start scoring – and there were consequences for whoever won/lost – then (in the scoring system) the pattern of who is playing well, and who is not playing well, takes on more meaning.

Knowing the current state of play, the current level of your performance, and the score has a significant impact on the thoughts, feelings, and behaviours of nearly all players. These may include nerves, frustration, anger, despair, elation, optimism, relief, embarrassment… all leading to a variety of thoughts – both positive and negative.

In this section, we will explore the scoring system, the effect of the scoring system on performance, and (therefore) its impact on the journey of the match.

# The scoring system

The original scoring system in badminton maintained that you had to win the right to serve and, therefore, the right to score a point. You were only able to score points on service. The games were played up to 15 points, but if you tied at 13-all, there was setting to 5 points; or if you tied at 14-all, there was setting to 3 points.

This led to very, very long matches(!) and long periods of time where nobody moved forwards on the scoreboard. In an attempt to make the sport more dynamic and spectator-friendly, the World Badminton Federation brought in rally point scoring, where you gain a point for every rally won. They also changed the number of points required to win a game. Various scoring systems have been adopted over the previous 20 years:

- Best of 5 games to 7
- Best of 5 games to 9
- Best of 5 games to 11
- Best of 3 games to 11
- Best of 3 games to 21

Many international badminton leagues have also experimented with new scoring systems such as the Indian Premier League (IPL), Danish League, German League, and the English National Badminton League (NBL). Each scoring system is devised to create continual flow and enable pressure points to occur more frequently. They all create different emotional and mental challenges for players.

In every match, the scoring system gift-wraps ideal opportunities for turning points to the player who is losing. The scoring system is what makes badminton such an unpredictable game, one in which the match is never finished until it's finished.

It is a scoring system that makes for great excitement because it is not time-restricted; a badminton match does not finish because the players have been playing for 90 minutes, and nobody can be quite sure where the finishing line is going to be.

# Implications

Firstly, if you are behind, *never give up*, no matter how badly you are playing. The scoring system can effectively be a *get out of jail* card because it's never too late to start playing well. This means your attitude is key. Poor play in a match can be forgotten as long as you keep a positive attitude. A positive attitude allows you to keep your mind open to seeing the opportunities the scoring system will present you with.

So, if you are the type of player who can't always guarantee being consistent (nearly all of us!), this is great news. Control what you can guarantee controlling – your attitude – and things could swing your way. If you are able to time your best play with the times when it matters most, then you'll always be able to create opportunities for yourself. For example, you may have played poorly but scored enough points to stay in touch, giving you opportunity to put together a run of points to surge through with momentum building for you.

Secondly, when you are in the lead, be aware that badminton will give your opponent chances they may well not deserve. Be ready to renew your efforts at these times. Do not let them take you by surprise; when they come along, respect the scoring system and be prepared to tackle any stings in the tail. With this positive attitude, these moments – like all potential turning points – can be well negotiated as you continue forward.

Earlier, we mentioned that the score presents you with opportunities; let's now look at *when* these opportunities occur.

# The score and potential turning points

While most potential turning points are unpredictable, those related to the score can be predicted. The scoring system provides the structure for the journey of the match. It provides a landscape against which we watch the game unfold.

If you take time to think about it, you will be able to identify the 'landmarks' within this landscape. These landmarks are landmarks because *you have seen them before*, and you know their potential significance and the impact they can have on the journey. These landmarks may represent a fork in the road, an easy part of the journey, a difficult part of the journey, or perhaps a good place for an ambush!

Badminton coaches often refer to *big points* – the idea being that some points are worth more than others. These points are those that give the best chance of turning the momentum in your favour. They are the times when only a few actual points played (or maybe even one point) have the best chance of affecting a player's energy and can thus change the match momentum. It is at these moments when a player has most to gain or most to lose.

These moments often occur during *critical periods*. It is usually as a result of what happens in these critical periods that surges of momentum can occur. If an opportunity is missed during a critical period, you will typically hear players and coaches say (afterwards) that it would have been a different match if that opportunity had been taken. What they mean is that the journey of the match from that point would have been different because of the effect it would have had.

There is, therefore, a strong link between potential turning points and the score because there are certain critical scorelines – or times in a match – when there is a distinct possibility that things could turn around, such as when the time comes to close out a lead, sometimes known as 'scoreboard pressure'.

As we have seen, the developing score can create a variety of thoughts, feelings, and emotions, which can all increase in intensity as these critical periods approach. In the matches where the biggest prizes are at stake, there are always these 'can they do it?' moments. Most top players are aware of them, but *when* are they and can you anticipate them?

## The start of the match

The start of the match is important. How you start sets the tone for the first set, and the first set sets the tone for the match. A set is clearly halfway to winning a three-set match, but we would argue that winning the first set is worth slightly more than this. This is because the effort to come back from losing a first set requires a player to win two sets back-to-back and – in terms of focus and physical exertion – that is twice as burdensome as if they had won the first set.

The GB Olympic Badminton team, in preparation for the 2008 Beijing Olympics, found that they were losing too many sets 21-18/21-17 and yet felt that they were competing admirably against their often Chinese and Korean adversaries. On closer tracking of the scorelines, a consistent theme emerged. They always had a poor start to the match, having a 3 or 4 point run against them early on in the game. For the rest of the match, the points were scored very evenly, but that 4-1 or 3-0 deficit at the start was transferring into a 21-18 loss. This was often the only 3-point run of scoring throughout the whole match. It became clear that we *had* to start matches much more focused and effectively as our Asian counterparts; they had clearly mastered that side to things.

We put together a plan which included 'dynamic warm-ups', which were more explosive and cognitive than previous warm-ups with lots of decision-making aspects. Our players had the challenge to win the first 5-point game within the game; in other words, they sought to establish a real mental focus on the start of the match. Within a very short period of time, this approach had a significant impact. We no longer had the luxury of being able to 'feel' our way into the match.

## Starting a new set

A new set is a new start. When a set is won or lost, it is easy to believe that the next set is bound to go the same way. In fact, the beginning of the next set gives you a great chance of a turning point. This is true of every start to a set, but let's look at them individually:

*Starting the first set*

The start of the match is important; as mentioned, it sets the tone for the first set and the subsequent atmosphere for the whole match. The start of the match is the first *opportunity* to establish the flow of the match in your favour. Get off on the wrong foot and you will have to make a change, so aim to get off on the right foot. This is done best by establishing your intentions – both tactical and mental – early on.

If you intend to attack in the match, then be positive and aggressive in your approach right from the beginning. If you intend to be the 'bigger personality' in the match, then show that right from the start with lots of positive energy. Whatever you intend, don't be slow coming out of the traps; momentum doesn't come your way if you wait for things to get going.

*Starting the second set*

The start of the second set is often critical. The score goes back to 0-0. We know you know this, but think about it. Imagine matches involving team sports (hockey, basketball, soccer, etc.) going back to 0-0 at the end of each half or quarter! Imagine a marathon when all the runners return to the start line after 13 miles!

If you have won the first set, then establishing a lead in the second suggests – to the opposition – that the established direction of the match will continue. Indeed, a set and 1-4 rarely produces a win for the person behind.

If you have lost the first set, then establishing a lead early in the second suggests the direction of the match may change. Whatever way the first set was lost, a lead shows your resilience to recover quickly. It shows that losing the first set is not so much of a setback that it diminishes your effort. In reality, it probably shows an opponent that you are mentally even stronger than before because they now face a player who has their belief boosted.

There are some additional factors that might work against the winner of the first set (and in favour of the one who lost). Many of these can catch out less-experienced players. For example, the airflow or drift in the arena can mean your shot power and precision has to be adjusted after a change of ends. Likewise, the vision of the shuttle can be quite different from end to end in many arenas, as can the crowd or the position of your support team. The environment is a key factor, and there is a skill in being able to adapt instantaneously.

In addition to these examples, the player who has lost the first set easily doesn't have to put full effort and concentration into the match until the start of the second set.

Conversely, the player who wins the first set has been concentrating for 15 minutes or so and now needs to continue at that level at the start of the second set, so the match doesn't turn around. They are unable to relax (even with a set in the bag). Even at 21-11, 12-12, although the score is numerically 33-23, it doesn't always feel like you have won 30% more points than the opponent.

It is worth looking in greater depth at some commonly occurring match examples:

*When the first set was 21-18*

If you lose a very closely-fought first game, and the momentum has gone against you, you can feel deflated as a result of *failing* when you were so close to establishing a lead. The second game can then very rapidly disappear before you have taken stock of the situation. By the same token, if you have just won a tight first game, if you can maintain the momentum and establish a mid-game lead at 11, you will often be well on your way to winning.

In both cases, you need to refocus and renew your efforts very quickly, but it is more urgent if you have lost the game. The scoreline 24-22, 21-10 is often seen (as mentioned in Chapter 2) as a result of the swing in momentum at the beginning of the second game. This is because a close gap in the level of play can become a large gap if both players change (i.e., one player's energy/confidence goes up, and the other's goes down).

In both situations, during your break at the end of the first set, you should review the game and decide what the best tactic to focus on – at the crucial start of the set – may be. You may or may not need to change tactics. If the first set loss was 24-22, it might be a question of only changing some minor things.

*When the first set was 21-10*

The score 10-21, 0-0 represents a great opportunity for a turning point for the player who has the momentum against them. Having lost the first game 10-21, you may feel down mentally, but if you can win the next few points, your mental energy will go up dramatically. The player who was winning 21-10 – but who then trails at 2-6 – may get frustrated by even such a minor change, and if it goes to 6-11, the match can be turned around by a swing in momentum.

If you won the first set 21-10, you need to be aware of the dangers of 0-0. Don't be daunted; it's how the scoring system works. The best approach is to treat a new set as a new start. Forget the last one, even though you won it easily, and start again. You need to start again in your mind because there is a difference from the last few points you played. During the last few points from 16 to 20, you had a big cushion and maybe tried for more *one-off* shots. Although you won the first game, at this reset of 0-0, you do not have the luxury of a big lead. From the opponent's point of view, they have to play well and play well now, so it is normal to expect an opponent to renew their efforts. Be ready for it but don't be fazed by it; for many players, the renewal of effort might only be a short-term thing unless they see a big swing in their favour. Things are likely to swing back your way if you don't panic, so hold your level and energy.

Whether you have won or lost the first set, you may need to prioritise the critical factors that underpin your competitive intensity. You may need to change tactics, or you may need to be more consistent with the ones you have.

*Starting the third set*

The start of the third set is another good chance for a turning point. If you have won the first set, but lost the second, you need to have a good start to the third to re-establish the momentum in your favour. Meanwhile, it may be the first chance you have had to get a lead in the score in the whole match if you lost the first set. If you win the first few points, the fact you hold the lead has an effect on the energy of both you and your opponent. Let it be seen in your body language that you are renewing your efforts and are psyched up for the decider.

If you have won the second set, you need to put it out of your mind and quickly refocus. Give your opponent the impression that things will continue in the same pattern as the second set. If you won a tight second set – where all the action was at the end – you might be fooled into relaxing, thinking that all the action will come at the end of the third. Of course, it might, but whoever refocuses quickest may win the set because they built a lead at the start of the final set. Be prepared for your opponent to start again and renew their efforts; they will if they are any good. Most of the principles that apply to the start of the third set also apply to the start of the second set.

After two sets, you should have a lot of information about which tactics work best. As with the examples above, at the end of the second, you should review the set and decide on the best tactic to employ at the start of the third set.

## Match point

You can be 18-21, 17-20 down, never having held the lead at any point during an hour of play, and yet able to save the match points and win the set. You are completely equal in the match, and the momentum is with you! In any team sport which is timed, the team in the lead could pack its defence and wait for the final whistle ... but this is never true in badminton. Match point down may represent the best opportunity you've had in the match so far.

For example, in the 2006 Malaysian Open Final where Lee Chong Wei was 13–20 down against Lin Dan in the final set, he saved 8 match points and won the game and match 23–

21. Likewise, Kidambi Srikanth of India has won matches on numerous occasions from being match point down, whilst Tai Tzu Ying of Taipei also has a great record. Looking at things from the opposite perspective, all of us – including the very top players – have lost matches having held match points!

*Lee Chong Wei of Malaysia.*

In badminton – towards the end of any set – everyone knows a major score will take place one way or the other. Being so close to winning a set and losing it, or being so close to losing it and then winning, will clearly have a significant impact. The trick – as always – is how players approach taking their opportunities and then how they *respond*.

As we have indicated throughout the course of the book, making decisions about the best way forward in any given situation – and especially on match or set points – requires clarity. This clarity stems from the journey of the match, including your tactical and mental observations and options. There is no quick fix or single answer we can give you that applies to all situations. For example, a top player may decide, on one occasion, to take a calculated risk on a match or set point based on their assessment of that match. In comparison, the following week, on a match/set point against a different opponent, they may decide to play safe, equally based on the assessment of the game at the time. Whatever the case, though, having a *considered* and *calculated* approach rather than a mindless and overly-emotional approach is what we'd recommend.

# Setting

In the current scoring system (2022), if the score reaches 20-20, then setting takes place. This may continue onwards to a score of 29-29 if nobody has reached two clear points, at which time the next point wins the set. Competitors need to be fully aware of their emotions and their tactical intentions in order to maximise their capabilities throughout setting. Setting sharpens the need for the speed at which players assess tactics and renew their efforts.

# Unscheduled breaks

Breaks for shuttle changes or court sweeps can have a big effect on the flow of a match. They can cause a change in energy in both players, which is often multiplied as time goes by and the match moves into its final stages. One player can take advantage of the fact they are still in the match and have time to regroup off court; the other can get frustrated and perhaps concerned that things might not go as well when play recommences.

During a regular towel break, players should use the time to regroup and maintain their focus using analytical thinking. Mentally, they should stay focussed, review tactics, and get ready to bring fresh energy to the court.

# Mid-game and end of game intervals

As discussed previously, mid-game and end of game intervals provide an essential opportunity for reflection and coach/athlete interaction. Whether you're a club player who never has a coach, or an Olympic athlete, it is important that you think through and agree on a plan to maximise any opportunity. You need your decision-making to be optimal; good decisions bring performance advantages over opponents.

Here's an insight into the detailed planning and thought that goes into Olympic-level badminton from Andy Wood:

# The Chair Strategy

In GB Badminton, we called this opportunity [coach/athlete interactions] the 'Chair Strategy'. The 'Chair' part referred to the fact that the coach was in the 'Coach's chair' courtside and was entitled to offer feedback verbally in-between points, and was also allowed onto court to communicate with their player at the mid-game and end of game intervals.

Every athlete requires a personalised approach in these scenarios, dependent on their psychological, emotional, and mental profiles and preferences. Accordingly, coaches must be capable of delivering in a multitude of different ways, and must be experts at sensing changes in their athlete's psychological and emotional states throughout the duration of the match. By recognising change, they can adjust their approach and delivery as required in order to optimise clarity and effectiveness.

In order to create the most effective 'Chair Strategy' the following must be considered:

PRE-MATCH.

How long before the match do I wish for the coach/athlete briefing to take place?

- Before my warm-up?

- After my warm-up?

- As soon as I enter the hall?

- The night before the match?

In turn…

Should there be a detailed tactical briefing the night before, and just a short reminder after the pre-match warm-up?

- Do I want to focus mainly on our side, and just a little on the opponent?

- Or do I want to know everything about the opposition? Do I want video clips on opponents' habits?

- Do I want a personalised motivational video?

- What is the approach and tone in delivery… is it calm and relaxed, or is it intense and motivational?

- Are we setting keywords or reminders for tactical plans, or just going with the flow?

Incidentally, getting all this in place and agreed *before* the match becomes even more important in doubles events when the two partners often have different preparation requirements or preferences. Some partnerships warm-up together and do everything together with full alignment; others prefer to warm up and prepare separately and don't come together until they both enter the court.

*Chair Communication Style*

Normally, two coaches are allowed on the coaches' chairs courtside. They can offer comments and encouragement verbally in-between points, as long as they don't delay the speed of play in any way.

There are roughly 10 seconds between points in badminton matches. Embroiled in fierce competition, players try to implement their in-between point routines as well as make decisions on their next play. On top of this, they may be trying to decipher and make sense of dialogue that they can only partly hear from an excited and emotionally-committed coach at the back of the court (or even two coaches shouting at the same time)! As you can see, it is important to figure out your very best communication method:

- Do we need communication or encouragement after every point?

- Or only occasionally because then we know it is important?

- Do we need to be calm, collected, and relaxed or fist-pumping and on fire!?

- Is one of the coaches offering tactics and the other purely motivational?

- Do we only talk if the match is not going as planned, or should there be constant reminders and reinforcement?

- Shall both coaches come onto court at the intervals or just one?

- Is it a signal when a player walks slowly in-between points around tramlines near the coach's chair that they want information?

- How do coaches react if an opponent or opponent's coaches are manipulating proceedings – stay calm and removed as the player can take care of it, or get involved to add force and back-up?

- How to react to poor officiating and line calls?

*Mid-game and end of game intervals*

Coaches should always consider the fact that they may have five opportunities – throughout a three-set match – to enter the court and impart assistance to their player(s).

Delivery across these five opportunities will need to be adjusted depending on the state of play, the journey of the match, and the athlete's interpretation (of where things stand), which dictates their response together with their current emotional and psychological states.

Break 1. 11 points in the first game – (1 min)

- Sense of calmness and relaxation

- Reinforce strategy

- Remind players of key points

- Initial view of opponent's real threats and capabilities as well as current form

- Deal with athlete's initial anxiety/adrenaline and transition into relaxed mid-game play and eliminate any fear


Break 2. End of the first game – (2 mins)

- Sense of calmness and reality

- First blows have been struck

- Formulate responses

- Actor or reactor

- Reinforce strategy

- Keyword reminders

- Reminder of change of end, arena challenges, (e.g., drift, vision, crowd)

Break 3. 11 points, mid-2nd game interval – (1 min)

- Sense of calmness, focus, and intensity
- Match revealing itself
- Sense of realisation – close out the match or fight to survive!
- Ensure clarity of thinking
- Assess acceptance levels

Break 4. End of Second game – (2 mins) Match completed or into final set decider.

- Sense of controlled urgency and high motivation
- Clarity established on opponent's threats, capabilities, and repeatable patterns now
- Ensure clarity in tactical adjustments and the challenge ahead
- Reinforce body language and need to impose self early in deciding game
- Reminder of change of end variables.

Break 5. 11 points, mid-3rd game interval – (1 min) Last chance saloon!

- Final opportunity for coach/athlete interaction, critical to maximise impact
- Match has revealed itself except for the pivotal deciding moments
- Approach-focussed intensity, high motivation, with a strong sense of trust and belief in player, instilling self-confidence
- Reminder of change of end variables
- Reminder of keywords and of playing the match at 'your' pace.

As you can see, there are endless considerations behind an optimal 'Chair Strategy' and every coach/athlete will require a custom, personalised approach. The more you prepare this, think it through, and visit every scenario, the more likely you are to respond in the right way at critical moments, under pressure, in the heat of battle.

# Key points

- Knowing the scoring system – and the opportunities/challenges it presents – is an integral part of being an effective match player.

- Match events can take on a greater significance at important scorelines.

- Match point-down might be your best opportunity to turn the match around.

- Have a clear plan for match and set points, based on match observations to that point.

- Have a strategy for your mid- and end of game intervals.

# Chapter 9: Bringing It All Together

## From training … to matches … to training … to matches

During the course of writing the book, when discussing our experience as coaches, it became obvious that our approach to performance coaching focussed on the integration of learning from training into match play and back to training as a *continuous learning journey*. This is because – at performance level – there are always significant competitions to build towards, which created overall annual plans and developed action plans for the players.

This continuing cycle of improvement does not lend itself to quick fixes and miracle drills on the training court. Nor does it lend itself to a programme which is heavily biased towards training, but which does not incorporate important lessons learned from matches.

There is a challenge here for many coaches who are not able to watch their players during matches. We have been very fortunate during our careers to often be on the road with players and therefore able to watch thousands of matches; over time, we have created a system which allows for common links and patterns to be seen from match to match which has allowed us to work on match-relevant skills.

As we have seen over the course of this book, there are very many variables which can affect players in matches and therefore, due to the variety of challenges, it is not easy to identify what to work on. The framework for understanding, and the ideas presented throughout the book, will (we hope) allow coaches and players to have a common language with which to discuss matches. From this, common situations and common skills to be worked can be identified. To help this, we have presented a framework for post-match reviews, which can be conducted, referring to the ideas and tools in the book, even if the coach has not been able to watch the match.

As we know, these skills fall into the tactical and mental areas of the game; we hope – by highlighting this – that our work will also have an impact on coaching sessions. They can easily become detached from the match court with an over-emphasis on technical skills in the mistaken belief that implementing refined techniques is the most important difference between winning and losing in matches.

If this was the case, we would see players who have the best technique smoothly moving from victory to victory. We know that this is not the case, and players are often required to win ugly when they turn up on a match court. When they turn up, they find their toolbox, which was full of tools only the day before on the practice court, now seems to contain fewer tools than they would wish for! This is why we have put such an emphasis in this book on critical thinking, seeing the bigger picture, and effective responses. These are skills that can be used to handle whatever situation you find yourself in, so that you can find different ways to win.

So, how can you ensure that you practice is focussed on developing from match to match? How can you ensure you are not making the same mistakes again and again in matches without working on them in practice? How can you take what is working well in matches and build on them to develop super-strengths?

The first step is to *identify your priorities* by taking stock of your current abilities, based on what we have covered in the book.

# Taking stock of your game

To help you assess where you are with your game right now, and identify areas of strength and areas for improvement, we have developed the Match Flow and Momentum Performance Profile. There's a copy below. Have a look at the profile and give yourself a mark for each. 1 is poor and 5 is excellent.

**Performance Profile**

| | 1 | 2 | 3 | 4 | 5 |
|---|---|---|---|---|---|
| **Control: Performance** | | | | | |
| You have a clear game identity | | | | | |
| You have a strategy to get your game in play at the start of the match | | | | | |
| You can assess the effectiveness of your game in a match | | | | | |
| You know how to maintain your performance when momentum is for you | | | | | |

| | 1 | 2 | 3 | 4 | 5 |
|---|---|---|---|---|---|
| You know how to adapt your performance when momentum is against you | | | | | |
| You know how to maintain/adapt your performance when it is in the balance | | | | | |
| You can review and explain your decisions in a post-match review | | | | | |
| | | | | | |
| **Control: Potential Turning Points** | | | | | |
| You can recognise potential points for you | | | | | |
| You can recognise potential turning points against you | | | | | |
| You know how to capitalise on potential turning points for you | | | | | |
| You know how to respond to potential turning points against you | | | | | |
| You know the windows of opportunity for potential turning points | | | | | |
| You can review and explain your choices in a post-match review | | | | | |
| | | | | | |
| **Big Picture Thinking** | | | | | |
| You know how to analyse the state of play | | | | | |
| You can assess your options | | | | | |
| You can make decisions based on the state of play | | | | | |
| You choose appropriate times to analyse the state of play | | | | | |
| You can implement decisions effectively | | | | | |

| | 1 | 2 | 3 | 4 | 5 |
|---|---|---|---|---|---|
| You can review and explain your choices in a post-match review | | | | | |

Having done the Performance Profile, why not you ask your coach to do it separately? Then arrange a meeting to go through each other's answers to discuss each item.

Once you have completed the above, identify three priority areas to work on and fill in the action plan below:

| Priority Area and Description: Main Aims | |
|---|---|
| 1 | |
| 2 | |
| 3 | |

Here are some examples for you:

Control Performance

- Know how to maintain/adapt performance when momentum is for you.
- Maintain momentum by sticking to the plan that got you into the winning position. As the Americans say, "Dance with the one that brought ya!"

Control Potential Turning Points

- Know how to capitalise on potential turning points for you
- Increase the success rate of taking opportunities from 1 out of 4, to 1 out of 3.

Big picture:

- Know when to use bigger picture thinking
- Become able to zoom out and check where you are in the match and if you're on the right track by assessing the state of play.

# Monitoring progress

Once you've established your priority goals, the next step is to work on improving them in practice and in matches.

It really goes without saying, but playing matches is the most important part of developing your match-effective skills! The best way to become better at playing matches is by playing matches! A coach once said that if you learn something in practice, you then have to wait and see if it works in a match, whereas if you learn it in a match... you save time!

Planning your tournament schedule or pre-season fixture list is important so you get the right balance between winning and losing. By this, I mean that a mix of easier and harder matches – to result in a 2 to 1 win/loss ratio – is the aim. By doing so, you retain confidence from the wins but can still identify areas to improve from both victories and losses. When it comes to high stakes, high emotion and high drama, it is very difficult to recreate the conditions of a match. That's why it's important to see matches as learning opportunities.

> "We never lost, we either
> won or learned."
>
> Clive Woodward

Setting goals pre-match and reviewing them post-match is a great way for you to take more responsibility and ownership. Not only does it encourage you to think clearly and objectively about your game, but it also encourages a more performance-focused mentality with an emphasis on specific goals within each match.

These reviews help players to strike a healthy mental balance between performance and outcome. The player who regularly sets pre-match goals then reviews their effectiveness after the match (post-match review), and is supported by feedback from their coach (match charts, video, etc), is giving themselves the best possible chance to improve.

Here's an example of a match review sheet:

| Date: | | Venue: | |
|---|---|---|---|
| | | | |
| Name: | | Opposition: | |
| | | | |
| Final Score: | | | |
| | | | |
| Priority Goals: | | | |
| | | | |
| Performance goals set prior to match (Achievement Rating 1-10) | | | |
| 1 | | | |
| 2 | | | |
| 3 | | | |
| | | | |
| Tips to help you achieve the above (Achievement Rating 1-10) | | | |
| 1 | | | |
| 2 | | | |
| 3 | | | |

# Match draw - a simple way to reflect on the match

An additional tool to help the match review is to draw (i.e., sketch) the match to see how it progresses from start to finish. In doing so, you will get a representation of the journey of the match, the different phases, and you can identify turning points.

This is done by drawing a line moving across a piece of paper (see below). Starting at the left in the centre of the page, you move across the page, *moving up* when momentum is for you and *down* when momentum is against you. The quicker that momentum swings, the steeper you draw the line.

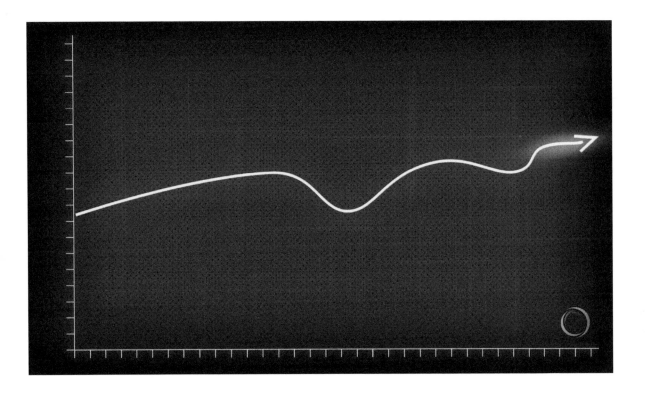

This can be used in the first instance as an educational tool and then – once you are familiar with it – it is an excellent way of reflecting on the match. A change in momentum (a turning point) can sometimes be pinpointed; for example, a missed opportunity or a change of tactics from a double substitution. It can also be used to identify times when you achieved a personal best when it comes to navigating the flow of the match.

Good practice is for the player to draw their version separately from the coach or observer, before comparing and contrasting the two versions to understand each other's perception of the match.

The key is to track elements of the performance from goals that were set pre-match, and not get side-tracked by the emotion often created by the final result. Identifying and agreeing what to measure is critical for this to be effective.

## Charting matches

This section is primarily for support staff (coaches/parents) to use whilst the player(s) is playing, although it can be done by the player(s) post-match – from a video – if they have one.

If you wish to take the Match Draw a stage further in detail, you can chart the momentum of a match and add layers of detail. There has been an explosion of the use of data in sport, and overall performance analysis is now a recognized career within sport. When done well, at the highest level, it can mean the difference between winning and losing.

Match analysis is used both for examining the weaknesses of the opposition, as well as for data-driven 'home team' coaching to identify strengths and weaknesses; in fact, it is becoming more and more the norm. Match analysis can reveal much, depending on the type of analysis. As with all data though, it is not the data – in itself – that is important, it is how it is analysed and then how it is presented for greatest impact.

There are many different ways of analysing matches and many of these methods result in a statistical analysis without the context of the match. They may not tell the story of the match, showing momentum changes or significant match events, as often they are averaged out across the match.

By comparison, the following two methods of momentum charting (described below), track the whole of the match, point by point, set by set, allowing players and coaches to see the *journey* of the match, and the state of play at any given point, as well as significant match events and reactions as events unfold. Some of these may be turning points; others may have been potential turning points.

## Method 1

This first example is more time-consuming and requires perhaps a greater focus on filling in the chart. As such, you can miss the feel for what is happening during a match because your head may be in the chart (a lot!). For this reason, especially when learning, it's better to do this method from a video of the match after it has taken place.

The second method is a more user-friendly method which allows for capturing the key points from the match without distracting from the play too much. It is therefore a good tool to use as events unfold.

For the first method, use an A4-sized piece of blank squared or graph paper and, starting at the centre line on the left-hand edge, mark a dot each time a point is won or lost (see graph). Mark the dot one square of graph paper up for each time your player wins the point; and one dot down for each time a point is lost. Continue the pattern until the end of each game, marking down the game score. Separate the games by a line and identify who is serving as the match continues.

The basic principle is that the chart records match events as they happen. The chart records both regular match events including the score, plus regular significant occurrences such as breaks in play, but also is flexible enough to record unpredictable match events which may turn out to be important such as referees' decisions or a sudden change in tactics by one side or the other.

This method allows the flow of points to be seen but can also be used to identify (or circle) certain key points or events. You may need to jot down a note so you can remember the point.

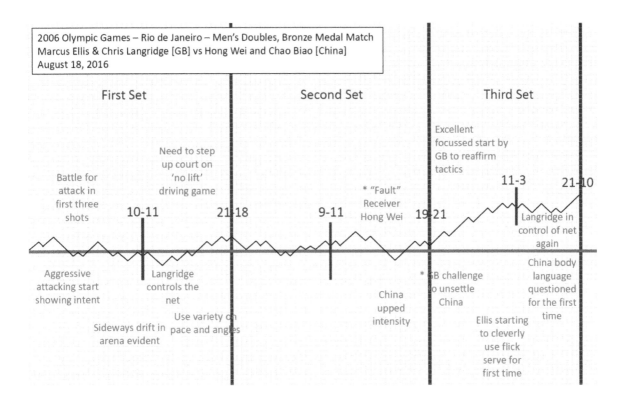

2006 Olympic Games – Rio de Janeiro – Men's Doubles, Bronze Medal Match
Marcus Ellis & Chris Langridge [GB] vs Hong Wei and Chao Biao [China]
August 18, 2016

**First Set**

Battle for attack in first three shots

10-11

Need to step up court on 'no lift' driving game

21-18

Aggressive attacking start showing intent

Langridge controls the net

Sideways drift in arena evident

Use variety of pace and angles

**Second Set**

9-11

* "Fault" Receiver Hong Wei

19-21

China upped intensity

**Third Set**

Excellent focussed start by GB to reaffirm tactics

11-3

21-10

Langridge in control of net again

China body language questioned for the first time

* GB challenge to unsettle China

Ellis starting to cleverly use flick serve for first time

## Method 2

The second method is one that was used by Great Britain's Olympic badminton team, some years ago.

It achieves most of the outcomes in the example above but additionally acts as an operational tool – mid-competition – to impart knowledge, clinically and effectively to athletes under stress. It also helps the coach to remain 'on track' with his/her messages.

In addition to this, it can be used as an information resource to other members of the multidisciplinary team, such as physiotherapists, strength and conditioning experts, nutritionists, etc, who don't normally travel (and are therefore not present) but who need to be kept aligned to performance planning and objectives. For this reason, competition Match Charts are copied and circulated amongst the team immediately.

Match charts can also contain W.I.P.S. – Work in Progress areas – so all members of the support team can have clarity on priority work areas. When used with the British Olympic team, short W.I.P.S. videos were produced for all athletes, identifying their immediate target areas for the next month ahead, with match clips highlighting the areas they needed to develop before the very next tournament. The Match charts would also identify 'Motivation' points denoted by a circle with an M in it. Each athlete also had consistently-produced personal motivational videos of themselves with career highlights of outplaying top international opponents, which they would use for their pre-match preparations and inspiration.

It is important to be clear on your purpose behind charting matches, and how it can support you with your intended coaching message or performance journey. Undoubtedly, the example below varied considerably at different times – depending on the stage of the athlete's performance journey and the information required – which resulted in different 'keys' as we captured slightly different information. The framework and the method, however, stayed the same.

Start in the top left-hand corner of the page with two vertical columns, entitled 'us' and 'them'. As a point is scored, write down the number of points accrued under the correct column (e.g., us or them).

Make notes of important events and align them to the score at which they occurred.

Decide on your 'key' and remember to use it.

Make sure you have a section at the top reminding you of your 'pre-match plan' and any potential match impactors.

Be sure to show any runs in points, and any thinking about what your first game interval coaching messages will be. Write them down.

Be mindful of identifying both W.I.P.S. and motivation clips.

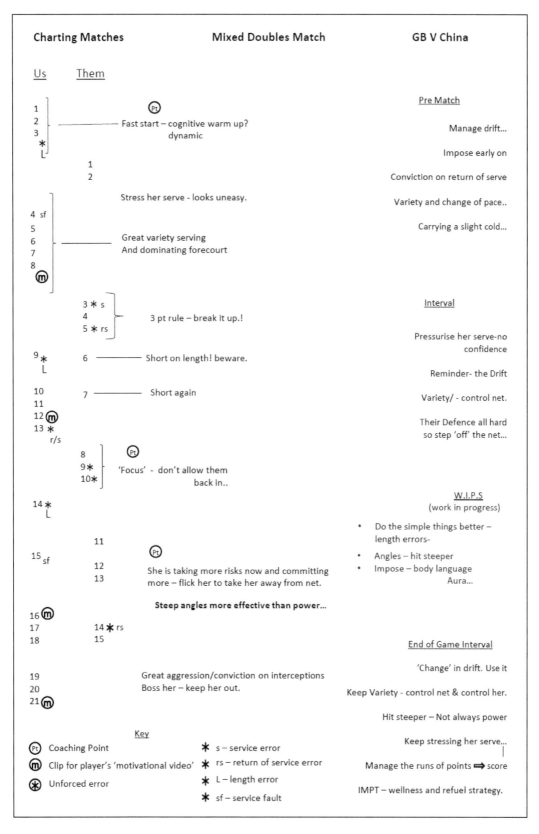

Charting Matches　　　　Mixed Doubles Match　　　　**GB V China**

Us　　Them

1
2　　　——————— Fast start – cognitive warm up?
3　　　　　　　　　　　dynamic
*
L

1
2

4 sf　　　　　Stress her serve - looks uneasy.
5
6　　　——————— Great variety serving
7　　　　　　　And dominating forecourt
8
ⓜ

Pre Match

Manage drift...

Impose early on

Conviction on return of serve

Variety and change of pace..

Carrying a slight cold...

3 * s
4　　　　 3 pt rule – break it up.!
5 * rs

9 *
L

10　　7 ——————— Short again
11
12 ⓜ
13 *
r/s

6 ——————— Short on length! beware.

Interval

Pressurise her serve-no
confidence

Reminder- the Drift

Variety/ - control net.

Their Defence all hard
so step 'off' the net...

8
9 *　　 ⓟᵗ　'Focus' - don't allow them
10 *　　　　　　　　back in..

14 *
L

11
15 sf
12　　 ⓟᵗ
13　　She is taking more risks now and committing
　　　more – flick her to take her away from net.

**Steep angles more effective than power...**

W.I.P.S
(work in progress)

• Do the simple things better –
　length errors-
• Angles – hit steeper
• Impose – body language
　　　　　Aura...

16 ⓜ
17　　14 * rs
18　　15

19　　Great aggression/conviction on interceptions
20　　Boss her – keep her out.
21 ⓜ

End of Game Interval

'Change' in drift. Use it

Keep Variety - control net & control her.

Hit steeper – Not always power

Keep stressing her serve...

Manage the runs of points ⟹ score

IMPT – wellness and refuel strategy.

Key

ⓟᵗ Coaching Point　　　　* s – service error

ⓜ Clip for player's 'motivational video'　* rs – return of service error

✱ Unforced error　　　　* L – length error

　　　　　　　　　　* sf – service fault

# Moving Forward

You are now armed with the knowledge you need to win more often! You have a deeper understanding of what to expect during competition and are better prepared for what matches can throw at you. You are now all set to use Match Flow, Momentum, and Turning Points to your advantage.

So why not start in your very next match? Let's have a closer look at how you can use what we have covered to gain the winning edge.

For your next match, have a clear idea of your own game, your own strengths and weaknesses. Visualise yourself on the court you will play on. How do you see yourself wining points? You can check back to Chapter 6 to be clear on your 'blueprint' tactical approach, then Chapter 7 to be clear on your 'blueprint' mental approach.

If you know the opposition you are playing, Chapter 7 will also help you to establish your own ranking system, so that you are in the best possible frame of mind to compete throughout the match, regardless of expectation.

That's a good start but is just pre-match and only focuses on your game. During your next match, if your opposition are worthy competitors, they will be looking to interfere with your pre-match plans!

During the match, you will have to make adjustments as the game progresses. In Chapter 6, we looked more closely at your tactical options and suggested some tactical thinking you can use. For example, as the match progresses you could reflect on who is the actor and who is the reactor, and perhaps consider whether you need to be more conservative or more adventurous with your play.

Your very next match will have a journey. By now, you know it's unlikely to progress from good, to very good, to great, to game over! It will go through different phases and contain significant match events. In Chapter 3, we described what these different phases of momentum can feel like for all players, and in Chapter 4 we suggested approaches you can use to control momentum during these phases, including how to keep yourself on an even keel mentally and make the best tactical decisions.

In Chapter 2, we gave you examples of match events which could become significant depending on your reaction, known as potential turning points which could become turning points. These are especially important when it comes to gaining maintaining or regaining momentum, as they have the ability to significantly impact how players are feeling about a match's progression, which can affect player performance. Revisit the second half of Chapter 5 on how to control potential turning points and be ready to respond effectively.

And of course, the scoreboard is going to change after every point. The score is important as it will present you with some opportunities and also some challenges. Chapter 8 covers what to expect and where you might be able to capitalise. But don't concentrate on the score, *focus on your performance*. Although the score will give you immediate feedback after every point, it is not always accurate feedback as you may perform brilliantly and lose the point. So, learn to assess your own performance and use that as feedback as to how well you are doing, rather than just the score. Your performance is more controllable than the score. Remember, it's the tactical and mental areas that you can consciously change during a match to control your performance and, therefore, control momentum.

In Chapter 5, we covered a simple way of thinking that you can use to establish the state of play and decide the best way forward based on what's happening in the game. Use this again and again to decide what it is that's making the difference, and therefore your best course of action as the match progresses. In your very next match, you could start by using this way of thinking during the breaks of play.

If you want to see how to structure thinking across a match, why not revisit the Olympic chair strategy that we covered in Chapter 8.

And, finally, remember that it's all about the gap in performance you can create between you and the opposition at critical times during the match. The gap builds momentum in your favour and you can benefit from a surge of momentum at a crucial time. Revisit Chapter 2 to see how we described this with the use of our battery graphics. Look for a way to create, widen, or close this gap in performance to gain the upper hand.

You won't get every decision right every time, but with the knowledge from this book, and from match to match, you will learn to control your performance and adapt your tactics and mental state to give yourself the best chance of winning. Good luck!

## ACT IN SPORT: Improve Performance through Mindfulness, Acceptance, and Commitment

ACT – Acceptance and Commitment Training/Therapy – is a modern and effective psychological approach based on a scientific understanding of human thought and emotional processes. ACT uses a practical and easy-to-use framework for skill development through values-based action, commitment, defusion, mindfulness, and acceptance.

By utilising ACT, athletes will flourish into their better selves and improve their performances across their sports and beyond.

## Tipping The Balance: The Mental Skills Handbook For Athletes

*Tipping The Balance* offers contemporary evidence-based and highly practical mental strategies that help an athlete to develop the crucial mental skills that enable them to thrive under pressure, perform consistently when it matters most, and enjoy the challenge of the big event.

This book is about empowering you – the athlete – no matter what level you perform at. In this book, you will discover the secrets of how the world's greatest athletes draw on cutting edge psychological skills to use what's between their ears to maximize performance.

## Master Your Chronic Pain: A Practical Guide

Do you want to manage your chronic pain and get your life back on track? Are you fed up with being held hostage by persistent pain and want to take action now? *Master Your Chronic Pain* adopts a holistic view of pain, looking at different aspects of pain management, from the benefits of mindfulness meditation to overcoming a fear of exercise to strategies for improving sleep. The emotional impact of pain is discussed, and practical tips for managing stress, worry, and low mood are given.

### Togetherness: How to Build a Winning Team

Togetherness is a powerful state of connection between individuals that can lead to amazing triumphs. In sport, teams win matches, but teams with togetherness win championships and make history. This concise and practical book – from Dr. Matt Slater, a world authority on togetherness – shows you how you can develop togetherness in your team. The journey starts with an understanding of what underpins togetherness and how it can drive high performance and well-being simultaneously. It then moves onto practical tips and activities based on the 3R model (Reflect, Represent, Realise) that you can learn and complete with your team to unlock their *togetherness*.

### The Honest Truth: Using the ACR to explore Alcohol Dependency

Alcohol dependency – where alcohol has a hold over someone's behaviour – affects people from all walks of life. It can impact an individual's health, wealth, relationships, life fulfilment, and so much more. In *The Honest Truth*, we explore how to evaluate whether someone has a dependency on alcohol through the ACR: the Alcohol Consumption Regime. It is a focused, simple, six-week programme punctuated with periods of permitted drinking and periods of non-drinking.

### Perform & Thrive: A Sportsperson's Guide to Mental Health and Wellbeing

How do sportspeople keep on top of wellbeing and the mental side to both sporting performances and life overall? In this book, by top Chartered Psychologist Sarah Broadhead, we deep dive into the elements that really count, and identify what can be done – practically – to provide sportspeople with the best possible chance of success. Filled with real-world examples, findings from the latest research, plus life stories from top athletes, this book – for athletes, coaches, and administrators – is a must-read for nurturing people who wish to perform and thrive!

Lightning Source UK Ltd.
Milton Keynes UK
UKHW051230131022
410364UK00001B/1